FAUNA AND FLORA

OF THE BIBLE

Helps for Translators Series

Technical Helps:

Old Testament Quotations in the New Testament
Short Bible Reference System
New Testament Index
Orthography Studies
The Theory and Practice of Translation
Bible Index
Fauna and Flora of the Bible
Manuscript Preparation
Marginal Notes for the Old Testament
Marginal Notes for the New Testament
The Practice of Translating

Handbooks:

A Translator's Handbook on the Book of Joshua
A Translator's Handbook of the Book of Ruth
A Translator's Handbook on the Book of Amos
A Translator's Handbook on the Books of Obadiah and Micah
A Translator's Handbook on the Book of Jonah
A Translator's Handbook on the Gospel of Mark
A Translator's Handbook on the Gospel of Luke
A Translator's Handbook on the Gospel of John
A Translator's Handbook on the Acts of the Apostles
A Translator's Handbook on Paul's Letter to the Romans
A Translator's Handbook on Paul's First Letter to the Corinthians
A Translator's Handbook on Paul's Letter to the Galatians
A Translator's Handbook on Paul's Letter to the Ephesians
A Translator's Handbook on Paul's Letter to the Philippians
A Translator's Handbook on Paul's Letters to the Colossians and to Philemon
A Translator's Handbook on Paul's Letters to the Thessalonians
A Translator's Handbook on the Letter to the Hebrews
A Translator's Handbook on the First Letter from Peter
A Translator's Handbook on the Letters of John

Guides:

A Translator's Guide to Selections from the First Five Books of the Old Testament
A Translator's Guide to Selected Psalms
A Translator's Guide to the Gospel of Matthew
A Translator's Guide to the Gospel of Mark
A Translator's Guide to the Gospel of Luke
A Translator's Guide to Paul's First Letter to the Corinthians
A Translator's Guide to Paul's Second Letter to the Corinthians
A Translator's Guide to Paul's Letters to Timothy and to Titus
A Translator's Guide to the Letters to James, Peter, and Jude
A Translator's Guide to the Revelation to John

HELPS FOR TRANSLATORS

FAUNA AND FLORA
OF THE BIBLE

Prepared in cooperation
with the Committee on Translations
of the United Bible Societies

Second Edition

UNITED BIBLE SOCIETIES
London, New York,
Stuttgart

Books in the series of Helps for Translators may be ordered from a national Bible Society or from either of the following centers:

United Bible Societies
European Production Fund
D-7000 Stuttgart 80
Postfach 81 03 40
West Germany

United Bible Societies
1865 Broadway
New York, NY 10023
U. S. A.

ISBN 0-8267-0021-7

ABS-1986-500-3,500-CM-3-08513

Contents

[v]

Introduction

For the Bible translator perhaps no aspect of his work is more complex, confusing, and time-consuming than the problems encountered in attempting to render satisfactorily the terms for different plants and animals of the Scriptures. Though there are a number of books which have been published concerning the fauna and flora of the Bible, most of these prove to be of relatively little help to the translator. In some instances these books simply contain too much information, and extracting what is specifically applicable to the translator's problems proves to be enormously difficult. Some treatments, especially those which are highly technical, deal so much with differences of scholarly viewpoints that the translator is often more confused than helped. In other instances no attempt is made to deal with some of the so-called "marginal" difficulties, for example, the use of such terms in figurative expressions--precisely the area in which the translator often encounters his most severe complications. In addition, many treatments of Biblical fauna and flora have inadequate illustrations, so that those who are participating in the translation program are not able to "picture" what the plant or animal would look like and therefore find it difficult to suggest a local equivalent.

In order to help translators deal with certain aspects of their problems of finding satisfactory equivalents, this special volume on the fauna and flora of the Bible has been prepared. As may be readily noted from the system employed in dealing with the various terms, the names of animals and plants are listed alphabetically in English, normally based on the Revised Standard Version of the corresponding Hebrew and/or Greek terms. The suggested interpretations or renderings are not, however, restricted to the equivalents employed as headings. Note, for example, the wide variety of usage under the term for owl.

Immediately following the general term is the scientific designation, or designations if two or more possible interpretations of a Hebrew or Greek term are involved, e.g. the treatment of chameleon, a suggested translation of a Hebrew term which may also refer to a barn owl. Wherever possible or relevant, both the genus and the species of plants and animals are given, but often only the genus is mentioned, since there may be no way of knowing precisely which species is involved. Furthermore, in many instances Hebrew and Greek terms designate classes of animals and plants rather than being names for particular species.

The third type of information is the corresponding Hebrew and/or Greek terms. In some instances there are a considerable number of words, as in the case of Hebrew terms for "goat," and wherever possible or relevant, an attempt is made to distinguish the various meanings involved.

Far more important than even the scientific nomenclature or the detailed listing of Greek and Hebrew equivalents is the next section under each term in which (1) the animal or plant is described, (2) any special peculiarities are listed (especially those which might be relevant in determining the meaning or usage of the Hebrew and Greek terms), (3) problems of identification are discussed (including the citing of scholarly evidence), and (4) features of appearance and behavior, helpful in explaining Biblical treatments (especially in figurative usage), are dealt with. In a number of cases there are also brief discussions of some critical problems, especially those involving historical evidence, for example, in the treatment of camel. This descriptive section is especially important to the translator and really constitutes the justification for this volume.

For some terms there are unusually complex problems. For example, in attempting to render behemoth (an English borrowing from Hebrew), it is suggested that in many contexts it would appear that hippopotamus would probably be the most satisfactory equivalent. On the other hand, in Job 40.15 such a translation would be quite ridiculous, for though most of the description which occurs in the following three verses may be said to fit the hippopotamus relatively well, the idea that his "tail becomes stiff like a cedar" is simply not appropriate, for the hippopotamus has a ridiculously small tail. Some persons have suggested that perhaps the crocodile would be a more logical equivalent, and this is what the New English Bible has used, but only by altering rather radically some of the syntactic structures, so that the crocodile "devours cattle as if they were grass" rather than "eating grass like an ox." This is, of course, only one of many difficulties which this volume considers.

The final section under each heading consists of a list of references, which are exhaustive if the term or terms are relatively infrequent; but if the occurrences are numerous the reader is referred to a concordance.

Insofar as possible this book on fauna and flora tries to anticipate the major problems which Bible translators face, but quite naturally not all the difficulties can be handled. Under sycamore, for example, it is clearly stated that this refers to a tree which belongs to the fig family (of which the mulberry is also a member). It does not state that the sycamore tree known generally in Europe and America, and which is such an appreciated shade tree, is in no way related to the Biblical sycamore. Furthermore, no attempt is made to resolve the many special problems which arise in individual contexts. For example, in speaking of the vine in John 15, one must attempt to find some corresponding plant which is pruned in order to bear more fruit. In many parts of the world there is simply no vine-like plant which is so treated. It should also be quite understandable that this book makes no attempt to deal systematically with all the problems of Biblical symbolism. For example, in speaking of gathering "figs from thistles" (or thornbushes), the specific identification of the fruit fig is not so important as the fact of getting delicious fruit from a troublesome bush which is never known to produce fruit of any kind. On the other hand, in Luke 13.7 the parable of digging around and fertilizing a fig tree so that it may have at least one more chance to produce fruit, may be regarded as being symbolically significant. At least for some exegetes this reference to the fig tree is an allusion to Israel. Problems such as these are treated in the various Translators Handbooks published by the United Bible Societies and really cannot be handled in detail in a volume such as this one, which is designed to provide general background information rather than specific solutions to particular problems.

The actual answers which translators may arrive at may differ quite widely. In some instances one may be able to employ a term for a related species. Owls, for example, are almost worldwide, and though the specific owl existing in Bible times may not occur in the region of the receptor language, one can always choose the local term for an owl which is more or less of the same size and behavior habits.

On the other hand, one may often have to employ a term for something belonging to quite a different species, but having some of the same essential features. For example, "cedar" in the Scriptures refers to a wood which was aromatic and greatly valued for construction. (In reality, the English term cedar is often, in current usage, applied to wood which is produced by cypresses, junipers, and even certain tropical trees completely unrelated to cedars.) Accordingly, many translators have employed a term which designates this type of prized timber (and the corresponding trees) rather than attempt to borrow a word such as cedar, which would not have meaning to the people.

Another solution may be a general descriptive equivalent. For example, in place of "behemoth" one may use a term such as "huge animal." Similarly, in talking about "wolves in sheep's clothing," some translators have used "fierce animals looking like tame animals." On the other hand, for this type of idiomatic saying, some languages already possess a well-established equivalent, e.g. "leopards looking like goats."

In some instances translators have avoided the problems of a specific term by reproducing only one of the relevant components of such a term. In Exodus 16.31, manna is likened to "coriander seed." It does not help the reader much to have one unknown substance, such as manna, likened to another unknown substance such as coriander seed. Hence, some translators have simply used a phrase such as "like small seed."

As already indicated, there is one more solution, namely, borrowing; and for a number of animals and plants of the Bible this is seemingly the only satisfactory solution. For example, most translators simply borrow a term such as camel, adapting it generally to the form of the word as used in the dominant language (often a trade or national language) of the area. Whenever such "zero" words are introduced into a text, there should be some marginal help, usually in a glossary.

Which of the various solutions a translator may feel is warranted in a particular instance will depend upon several factors. For one thing, he must carefully consider the existing tradition in translating, that is, the practice of other translations of the Scriptures into this receptor language. Of course, if the Bible is being translated into a language for the first time, one is in a sense freer to experiment, but only up to a point, for in all such instances there is normally some relatively well-established tradition in the dominant trade or national language of the area, and more often than not any "new language" must conform to the patterns which have already been accepted as theologically valid.

Another factor influencing the type of solution which a translator employs is the degree of cultural proximity to the Biblical life and times. For example, a translator in East Africa can often approximate the fauna and flora of the Scriptures quite closely, for there are so many animals and plants which are alike and so many cultural attitudes toward these which are similar.

One must, however, also reckon with the factor of degree of cultural insecurity possessed by the people speaking a particular receptor language. If such people are quite insecure, they are often likely to demand very close adherence to the literal forms of the Biblical expressions and terms. They frequently prefer to have borrowed words which they do not understand rather than venture to employ terms which may designate related, but not exact, equivalents. Anything less than what is "technically correct" may be interpreted by such persons as being a case of paternalism.

In cases in which the speakers of a receptor language are very sophisticated in their knowledge of the world and the differences which exist, one can also employ quite technical equivalents, but what may seem perfectly understandable to educated people may be utterly unintelligible to the masses. One must, therefore, always proceed with caution in using highly specialized vocabulary.

At the same time, what one places in the text of a translation will depend in very large measure on what one is prepared to place in the footnotes or in the glossary. The Bible Societies generally regard the publication of Scriptures without adequate marginal helps as a serious deficiency. They, therefore, want to encourage the introduction of marginal helps dealing with historical backgrounds and cultural differences which may be essential for a satisfactory understanding of the text. A glossary of some two hundred words is usually a necessity and an average of between one and two marginal notes per page is usually required if people are to comprehend the setting in which the Biblical events took place and if they are to appreciate the cultural differences which contribute so much to the meaning of the message.

The United Bible Societies are much indebted to the Rev. Dr. K. E. Jordt Jørgensen for the basic research which went into the preparation of this volume. Moreover, the Danish Bible Society is to be especially thanked for its wholehearted support of this program during the several years in which it was being carried out. Special thanks is also due to the Rev. Clifford Culshaw for his careful editing and verification of the section on flora. It has been especially useful to have in the preparation of this volume the collaboration of the artists who have prepared the excellent illustrative drawings: Mr. G. W. Smith for the section on fauna and Mrs. U. Lollesgaard for the section on flora. Thanks are due to Mrs. J. Sheffield and especially to Miss Edyth Banks for preparing the final form of the manuscript.

Even though this volume cannot be expected to provide automatic answers to all the problems of fauna and flora which the Bible translator faces, nevertheless, it should go a long way in providing the indispensable background information on the basis of which intelligent decisions can be made.

INTRODUCTION TO THE SECOND EDITION

A number of translators and scholars have indicated the need for other indexes in addition to the Index of English and Latin Terms that was included in the first edition of this work. Therefore this second edition includes indexes of Greek, Hebrew, and Aramaic terms, of terms in certain other languages, and of Bible references.

We are much indebted to the following people who have contributed to the compilation of these indexes: René-Péter Contesse, Harold W. Fehderau, and H.W. Hollander. Thanks are due to Paul C. Clarke, Gloria Horowitz, Errol F. Rhodes, and Dorothy Ridgway for their part in editing and preparing the final form of the indexes.

Abbreviations

BOOKS OF THE BIBLE

Although not all of the 66 books of the Bible are referred to in this work, we list them in order here with their abbreviations:

Gn	Genesis	Na	Nahum
Ex	Exodus	Hbk	Habakkuk
Lv	Leviticus	Zeph	Zephaniah
Nu	Numbers	Hg	Haggai
Dt	Deuteronomy	Zech	Zechariah
Jos	Joshua	Mal	Malachi
Jg	Judges	Mt	Matthew
Ru	Ruth	Mk	Mark
1 S	1 Samuel	Lk	Luke
2 S	2 Samuel	Jn	John
1 K	1 Kings	Ac	Acts
2 K	2 Kings	Ro	Romans
1 Ch	1 Chronicles	1 Co	1 Corinthians
2 Ch	2 Chronicles	2 Co	2 Corinthians
	Ezra*	Ga	Galatians
Ne	Nehemiah	Eph	Ephesians
Es	Esther	Php	Philippians
	Job*	Col	Colossians
Ps	Psalms	1 Th	1 Thessalonians
Pr	Proverbs	2 Th	2 Thessalonians
Ec	Ecclesiastes	1 Ti	1 Timothy
SS	Song of Solomon	2 Ti	2 Timothy
Is	Isaiah		Titus*
Je	Jeremiah	Phm	Philemon
La	Lamentations	He	Hebrews
Ezk	Ezekiel	Jas	James
Dn	Daniel	1 P	1 Peter
Ho	Hosea	2 P	2 Peter
	Joel*	1 Jn	1 John
Am	Amos	2 Jn	2 John
Ob	Obadiah	3 Jn	3 John
Jon	Jonah		Jude*
Mi	Micah	Rv	Revelation

* To avoid possible confusion with other books and because these books are not frequently referred to and the names are short, these are not abbreviated.

OTHER ABBREVIATIONS

AG   Arndt-Gingrich Lexicon*
AV   Authorized (King James) Version of the Bible
BDB   Brown-Driver-Briggs Lexicon*
BHH   Biblisch-Historisches Handwörterbuch*
HDB   Hastings Dictionary of the Bible*
ID   Interpreter's Dictionary of the Bible*
JB   Jerusalem Bible
KB   Koehler-Baumgartner Lexicon*
LXX   The Septuagint
NEB   New English Bible
NT   New Testament
OT   Old Testament
OTTP   Old Testament Translation Problems (Hulst)*
RSV   Revised Standard Version of the Bible
RV   Revised Version (British) of the Bible

cf	compare, see also	m	metre(s)
cm	centimetre(s)	mg	margin
Gk	Greek	p	page
Hb	Hebrew	v	verse
kg	kilogram(s)	vv	verses

* For further information on these works, see the Bibliography, pages 199-201.

System of Transliteration from Hebrew

א	ʾ	ח	ḥ	פ	p
ב	b	ט	ṭ	ף, פ	ph
ב	bh	י	y	ץ, צ	ts
ג	g	כ	k	ק	q
ג	gh	ך, כ	kh	ר	r
ד	d	ל	l	שׂ	s
ד	dh	ם, מ	m	שׁ	sh
ה	h	ן, נ	n	ת	t
ו	w	ס	ṣ	ת	th
ז	z	ע	ʿ		

System of Transliteration from Greek

α	a	ι	i	ρ	r
β	b	κ	k	ς, σ	s
γ	g	λ	l	τ	t
δ	d	μ	m	υ	u, y
ε	e	ν	n	φ	ph
ζ	z	ξ	x	χ	ch
η	ē	ο	o	ψ	ps
ϑ	th	π	p	ω	ō

Fauna of the Bible

Ant   Messor semirufus

Hebrew: nemalah

DESCRIPTION: The ant in question is the harvester ant, Messor semirufus, which is to be found everywhere in Palestine. It stores grain within its nests, and is therefore used as an illustration of industry, but it also causes much damage to farmers.

REFERENCES: Pr 6.6; 30.25

Ants (*Messor semirufus*)

Antelope   Antilope addax, Oryx leucoryx

Hebrew: dishon

DESCRIPTION: The clean and unclean animals contained in the cat-
alogues of Lv and Dt are usually very difficult to identify. This is
true of the Hb dishon. AV follows LXX and renders it 'pygarg',
which literally means a white rump and is the Gk name of a kind of
antelope. Because of this Gk name, it seems reasonable to connect
the animal in question with the Antilope addax, a native of North
Africa, which has greyish-white hinder parts, a white patch on the
forehead and twisted and ringed horns.

Antelope (*Antilope addax*)

[2]

Antelope (*Oryx leucoryx*)

RSV translates 'ibex', but according to Bodenheimer this is a mistake. He is inclined to identify the dishon with the Arabian oryx, Oryx leucoryx, the biggest antelope of Iraq, which inhabits the deserts of Arabia and great parts of Africa and has characteristic long horns stretching straight backwards. Bodenheimer argues from the similarity between the Hb word dishon and the Akkadian da-as-su, which is the Arabian oryx.

JB has 'antelope' and NEB 'white-rumped deer'. RSV and NEB have 'antelope' for te?o in Dt 14.5 and Is 51.20. See IBEX.

REFERENCE: Dt 14.5

[3]

Ape simiæ

Hebrew: qoph, tukki

DESCRIPTION: Apes are mentioned only once in the Old Testament
and without definite description, so that a specification is mere
guessing. Apes were listed among the goods imported by the luxury-
loving King Solomon on board his mighty mercantile fleet. Bodenheimer points out that the reference in the same verse to 'ivory'
makes East Africa most probable as the exporting area, so that the
old translation of tukkiyim as 'peacocks' is most unlikely. He follows Albright, who identifies the Hb tukki with an Egyptian word ky
meaning a species of ape, just as qoph is to be identified with the
Egyptian gf, another kind of monkey. For the RSV translation, see
OTTP, p 38. JB has 'apes and baboons', NEB 'apes and monkeys'.

Feliks in BHH points out that in Ancient Egypt, as in Palestine
at the time of the Mishna, guenons (long-tailed monkeys, Cerco-
pithecus pyrrhonotus) and baboons (Papiobabuin) were kept as domestic animals. An old Egyptian picture shows a man carrying ivory and
a lion hide, with a baboon on a leash. The picture is part of a larger
illustration representing tribute being paid to Pharoah from the
Southern countries.

REFERENCES: 1 K 10.22; 2 Ch 9.21

Arrowsnake Otus scops (?) Eryx jaculus (?)

Hebrew: qippoz

DESCRIPTION: Many commentators now translate this Hb word
'arrowsnake' (so RV). The arrowsnake is a serpent which is able
to coil itself back and dart forward quickly like an arrow, or to
leap from a tree. The translation 'arrowsnake' has a long tradition
and is linked with the Aramaic root qaphaz, 'to leap, spring'.

ID finds it advisable to translate 'owl' like AV and RSV, following the suggestion made by Houghton, quoted in BDB under qippoz,
that 'the arrowsnake does not incubate' (the word baqe'ah used in

[4]

Is 34.15 means 'to hatch'), but whether Isaiah is to be credited with such accurate knowledge of natural history is questionable. JB has 'viper'.

Driver in HDB suggests that qippoz may be a variety of the sand partridge Caccabis sinaica (so NEB).

REFERENCE: Is 34.15

Ass Equus asinus   **Wild Ass** Equus hemionus

Hebrew: ḥamor, 'ayir (male ass), ?athon (she-ass) pere? (wild ass), 'arodh, 'aradh (Aramaic for wild ass)

Greek: onos, onarion (little donkey), pōlos (colt or ass's foal), hupozugion (beast of burden, ass)

DESCRIPTION: The European ass of today cannot be compared with that of the Orient. The domestic asses of Europe are usually small, stubborn and malicious animals, often considered stupid. In the East the ass develops into a beautiful, stately and lively animal.

The colour of the ass in the Middle East is usually reddish brown, which must also have been its colour in Biblical times, as indicated by the Hb word ḥamor, derived from the root meaning 'to be red'. An allusion to the colour may be found also in Jg 5.10, 'you who ride on tawny asses', translating tsaḥor as 'tawny' (RSV and NEB. AV and JB have 'white').

The story of Balaam (Nm 22) serves as an illustration of the ass's character. The ass sees the angel of the Lord, whom Balaam does not see, and halts each time. Balaam in his blindness beats his animal and rebukes it. Finally the ass begins to talk and says (v 30): '"Am I not your ass, upon which you have ridden all your life long to this day? Was I ever accustomed to do so to you?" And he said, "No".' This is not a description of a foolish or stubborn animal.

The ass was used as a mount from early times. Until the days of King Solomon the horse was not used in Palestine. But from that time

Wild ass (*Equus hemionus*)

on it was ridden by the warrior, whereas the ass was used by those who were travelling peacefully, like the king of peace (Zech 9.9) and Jesus entering Jerusalem (Mt 21).

The ass was also the Israelite's beast of burden, and its frugality and staying power made it more useful in that country than the horse or even the camel. After the return of the people from Babylonia we find that the statement of stock numbers ten times as many asses as horses and camels (Ezra 2.66-67; Ne 7.68-69). 'Ox and ass' is an almost proverbial expression for the domestic animals at the time of Jesus (Lk 13.15; cf Lk 14.5).

The ass was also used as a working animal, e. g. in grinding mills. The word 'millstone' used in Mt 18.6 and Mk 9.42 literally means 'a millstone worked by donkey power' (mulos onikos).

REFERENCES: ḥamor: Consult a concordance
'ayir: Gn 32.15; 49.11; Jg 10.4; 12.14; Job 11.12; Is 30.6, 24; Zech 9.9

[6]

?athon: Consult a concordance
pere?: Gn 16.12; Job 6.5; 11.12; 24.5; 39.5; Ps 104.11;
   Is 32.14; Je 2.24; 14.6; Ho 8.9
'arodh: Job 39.5   'aradh: Dn 5.21
onos: Mt 21.2, 5, 7; Lk 13.15; 14.5 (some MSS); Jn
   12.15
onarion: Jn 12.14
pōlos: Mt 21.2, 5, 7; Mk 11.2, 4, 5, 7; Lk 19.30, 33, 35;
   Jn 12.15
hupozugion: Mt 21.5; 2 P 2.16

DIFFICULT PASSAGES: Job 11.12: It seems evident that this verse is a proverbial saying (Weiser): No one can expect wisdom from a stupid man, any more than a wild ass can be expected to become a man. The Hb word pere? is translated 'zebra' by Weiser (following KB). JB has 'a young wild donkey grows tame'.

Undoubtedly the parallelism of Zech 9.9, 'riding on an ass, on a colt, the foal of an ass', has become the reason why Jesus, according to Mt 21.2, asks for an ass and a colt, although he needs only one mount. He wishes to point out that he is now bringing about the fulfilment of that old and cherished prophecy. Not that Jesus meant that Zechariah was talking about two separate animals; he wanted rather to show that the literal agreement between his own command and the poetical form of the prophet's words would prove that no mere coincidence but God himself was directing the steps of the Messiah. The difficulty of the double autōn in v 7, 'they put their clothes on them, and he sat on them', has made some commentators explain that Jesus was riding on each animal in turn. On this see Zahn, who reads auton instead of the first autōn: 'they put their clothes on it (the animal) and he sat on them (the clothes)'.

Bat Chiroptera

Hebrew: 'aṭalleph

DESCRIPTION: In the Law of Moses the bat is listed among the unclean birds; but it belongs to the mammals. It is a quadruped which

[7]

Bat (*Chiroptera*)

suckles its young. The 'wings' are membranes connecting the fore and hind legs.

The Hb name is used in general for all the many species of bats in the area. Modern zoologists have counted some twenty different species in Palestine alone. There does not seem to be any doubt about the identification in view of the allusion to the creature's haunts in Is 2.20: on the day of the Lord the idols will be cast forth to the bats, i.e. into ruins and caves.

REFERENCES: Lv 11.19; Dt 14.18; Is 2.20

Bear Ursus syriacus

Hebrew: dobh   Greek: arkos

DESCRIPTION: The Syrian bear which today may be found in the mountains of Lebanon and Anti-Lebanon is brown in colour and may reach a length of two metres and a weight of up to 250 kilos. Its food consists of vegetables, roots, grass, berries, fruits, nuts, honey and ants. In cases of emergency it also feeds on game, oxen, sheep or horses. The bear may be dangerous to man if provoked or 'robbed of her cubs' (2 S 17.8).

The bear and the lion are often mentioned together in the Bible (e. g. 1 S 17.37) as they are the two largest and strongest beasts of prey. They may thus symbolize strength and terror (e. g. Am 5.19). Isaiah uses the growl of the bear to illustrate the impatience of the Jews: 'We all growl like bears' (59.11). The paws of the bear sometimes serve as a dangerous weapon; this furnishes a clue to the inner meaning of the vision in Rv 13.2.

REFERENCES: <u>dobh</u>: Consult a concordance
                     <u>arkos</u>: Rv 13.2

Bear (*Ursus syriacus*)

Bees (*Apis fasciata*)

Bee   Apis fasciata

Hebrew: debhorah

DESCRIPTION: The way in which the Bible compares bees with an army chasing and surrounding man suggests the species still common in Palestine, Apis fasciata, which is very inclined to sting.

The honey of wild bees is often referred to (e.g. Mk 1.6), but there is no indication in the Bible of bee-keeping (known in Egypt from 2400 BC), except perhaps in Is 7.18, where the reference to hissing (AV) or whistling (RSV, JB, NEB) for bees may suggest that

Hornet (*Vespa orientalis*)

[10]

a bee farmer could cause bees to swarm by this procedure (so Brockington in HDB). Wild bees lived in rocks and woods.

The word debhash may not only signify bee honey, but also the honey or syrup extracted from such fruits as figs, dates and grapes. 'A land flowing with milk and honey' (Ex 3.8) thus does not stand for a land of bees, but a land rich in fruit.

REFERENCES: Dt 1.44; Jg 14.8; Ps 118.12; Is 7.18

DIFFICULT PASSAGE: 1 S 14.26: Instead of helek debhash 'the flowing of honey', some read halak debhorim 'its bees had flown away', cf JB 'the swarm had gone'.

Behemoth perhaps Hippopotamus amphibius

Hebrew: behemoth

DESCRIPTION: The head of the hippopotamus is almost quadrangular; its highly developed sense-organs are placed in such a way that the animal can see, hear and smell almost without being seen, because its eyes, ears and nostrils can reach above the water while the rest of the animal lies submerged in the river. Its mouth is enormous, with tusks reaching a length of 70 cm, and its throat is short and heavy. The legs are unusually strong and short, so that its belly almost reaches to the ground when the animal is on land.

The hippopotamus spends most of its time in the water where this apparently clumsy animal moves with great agility.

It lives on the grass and herbs that grow in the river, and if it does not find enough food there it comes on land. In spite of its heavy body the hippopotamus is also quite agile on land, even on steep and high banks. It usually comes ashore at night, but in daylight nobody can avoid noticing where it has been, as it tramples everything in its path. Lotus plants and other herbage along the river Nile are consumed in large quantities by hippopotami.

[11]

REFERENCES: Lv 11.2; Job 40.15; Ps 73.22; Is 30.6 etc.
Consult a concordance

DIFFICULT PASSAGES: Job 40.15: behemoth is originally the plural of behemah 'wild beast', and in this passage probably should be
translated accordingly.

One reason for rendering the Hb word 'hippopotamus', as many
modern translators do, is that the Hb may be derived from an Egyptian word p-ih-mw which is supposed to mean 'the ox of the water'.
But the existence of this Egyptian word is problematical. Further,
there are two difficulties in connection with the detailed description
of the animal in Job 40. One is v 17, 'He makes his tail stiff like a
cedar', which does not apply to the ridiculously short tail of a hippopotamus. Also, the mention of the sinews and bones of the animal in
v 17f is not appropriate, as the very thick hide of the hippopotamus
makes it impossible to discern what is beneath.

It is therefore advisable to translate Job 40.15 'wild beast'. NEB
has 'crocodile'. Lv 11.2, Ps 73.22 and Is 30.6 etc. should be translated 'beasts'.

Birds of prey

Hebrew: 'ayiṭ

DESCRIPTION: The Hb word may be derived from a root which
means 'to scream' or 'to shriek'. In general it may be said that
specification of the birds of prey mentioned in the Bible is difficult. Probably the authors of the Old Testament did not always
distinguish between them, though in cases when some kind of
description is to be found, it may be possible to do so. See VUL-
TURE.

Bodenheimer has listed thirty-three species of birds of prey
which have been found mummified in Egypt.

REFERENCES: Gn 15.11; Job 28.7; Is 18.6; 46.11; Je 12.9; Ezk 39.4

[12]

Camel (*Camelus dromedarius*)

Camel   Camelus dromedarius

Hebrew: gamal, bekher and bikherah (young camel);
        plural: kirkaroth

Greek: kamelos

DESCRIPTION: The camel belongs to the ruminants but has no cloven hoof. The feet have cushion-like soles enveloped in hardened skin. On Shalmaneser's obelisk (now in the British Museum in London) one may see a portrait of the two-humped camel (Camelus bactrianus) which is bigger, heavier and slower than the one-humped (C. dromedarius).

[13]

The camel has been called 'the ship of the desert', and it is true
that this animal is by nature adapted for life in desert regions.
This is not only because of its feet, but also because of its stomach
which holds water cells and may serve as a reservoir lasting several days. The hump with its reserve store of fat also makes it
possible for the animal to subsist on very little food during a desert
journey.

The original home of the camel was among the eastern neigh-
bours of Palestine, the Midianites, the Amalekites and 'all the people of the East' (Jg 7.12). A well-fed beast of burden can carry up
to 250 kg. This makes the description of the glory of the Jerusalem
to come the more impressive (Is 60.6) and is an indication of the
wealth of Abraham (Gn 24.10).

Camel hair was used for tents and sometimes for clothes (Mk 1.6).

REFERENCES: gamal: Consult a concordance
bekher: Is 60.6
bikherah: Je 2.23
kirkaroth: Is 66.20 (RSV, JB, NEB: 'dromedaries')
kamelos: Mt 3.4; 19.24; 23.24; Mk 1.6; 10.25;
Lk 18.25

DIFFICULT PASSAGES: Mt 19.24 (and parallels), a proverbial saying which compares one of the largest animals, the camel, with one
of the smallest openings, the eye of a needle, in order to underline
how difficult, not to say impossible, it is for man to break away
from earthly goods. A similar paradox is used by Jesus in his warn-
ing against the Pharisees who 'strain out a gnat and swallow a camel'
(Mt 23.24). The gnat is one of the smallest insects, and Jesus is
alluding to the habit of filtering wine before drinking.

Gn 12.16 says that for Sarah's sake Abraham was given camels by
Pharoah. But Dalman and Procksch comment that camels were not to
be found in Egypt at that time (see also Ex 9.3), but only much later,
at the time of the Persian wars. Either the author of this chapter is
mistaken, or Pharoah must have imported his gift. (Bodenheimer
states that the camel is an anachronism in the patriarchal stories.)

Chameleon (*Chamæleo vulgaris*)

Chameleon   Chamæleo vulgaris   **Barn Owl**   Tyto alba

Hebrew: tinshemeth

DESCRIPTION: We deal with these two in the same article, because they represent two different translations of the same Hb word.

In Lv 11.30 AV and Luther translate tinshemeth 'mole'. In our time scholars are more inclined to consider it to be the chameleon (so RSV and NEB. JB transliterates 'tinshameth'). The reason is, in the first place, that it is listed among the reptiles, and the chameleon belongs to the same order as the lizards. In the second place, the Hb name is derived from a verb nasham 'to pant'. The lungs of a lizard are very large, and Pliny's Natural History (8, 51) proves that in ancient times lizards were believed to live on air.

One peculiarity of the chameleon is its power to change colour according to its surroundings. Its eyes move independently of each other, and it may at the same time turn one eye upwards and the other downwards. In Palestine the chameleon lives in trees and bushes, clinging to the branches with its long tail.

JB translates ḥomeṭ as 'chameleon'. See LIZARD.

Lv 11.18 and Dt 14.16 deal with a bird. AV follows Vulgate in rendering 'swan'. Today zoologists suggest Athene noctua, the little owl (so NEB), or Tyto alba, the barn owl, the breathing of which sounds like snorting and thus gives an explanation of the Hb name. RSV has 'water hen', JB 'ibis'.

REFERENCES: Lv 11.18, 30; Dt 14.16

Cock (*Gallus domesticus*)

Cock, Hen, Chicken   Gallus domesticus

Hebrew: sekhwi, zarzir

Greek: alektōr (cock, rooster), ornis (hen), nossia (brood of chickens), nossion (chicken)

DESCRIPTION: Poultry farming originated in India, whence it spread to Babylon, Egypt, Greece and Palestine.

According to the Talmud (Strack-Billerbeck I, 992), the Jews were forbidden to have poultry in Jerusalem, because insects and larvæ from the dung might contaminate the meat which was used for offerings in the Temple. The references in the Gospels may therefore allude to cocks and hens kept by the Romans. Two Hb seals from Palestine, however, portray a rooster and make it certain that this fowl was found in Biblical lands in the first millennium BC.

The beautiful illustration used by Jesus of a hen gathering her brood under her wings (Mt 23.37; Lk 13.34) indicates that the domestic hen was kept at least in some places in Jerusalem at that time.

The cock's habit of crowing during the night made it a sign of the time, so that the third of the four Roman night-watches (12 to 3 a.m.) was named 'cock-crow' (Mk 13.35).

REFERENCES: sekhwi: Job 38.36
       zarzir: Pr 30.31
       alektōr: Mt 26.34, 74, 75; Mk 14.30, 68, 72;
        Lk 22.34, 60, 61; Jn 13.38; 18.27
       nossia: Lk 13.34
       nossion: Mt 23.27

DIFFICULT PASSAGES: Job 38.36: The significance of the word sekhwi is doubtful. There is a tradition for translating it 'cock' as in JB (Vulgate and one of the Targums). It may be derived from a root meaning 'to look out, watch, hope for', because the habit of announcing the coming of the day was attributed to the cock. Others translate 'appearance', which in this connection would mean northern lights, shooting stars etc., viewed as indications of the weather. RSV 'mists', NEB 'secrecy'. See also OTTP, p 89.

Pr 30.31: The word zarzir means 'one who is girt around the loins'. Some translators have 'cock' (Zürich Bible, JB, RSV and NEB), following LXX, Syriac and the Targum, and some take it to be another animal, e.g. a greyhound or war horse. The text is probably corrupt (as suggested by Kautzsch).

Cormorant (*Phalacrocorax*)

Cormorant   Phalacrocorax

Hebrew: shalakh

DESCRIPTION: The cormorant frequents swamps around the Sea
of Galilee, Lake Huleh and the Mediterranean coast, where it builds
its nest in high trees, usually in large colonies. It is a dark-
coloured bird with a rather long neck. Under the bill it has a sac in
which it keeps the captured fish. The Hb name originally denotes
the 'hurling down' of the bird upon its prey, illustrating its habit of
diving into deep water and sometimes practically swimming beneath
the surface in its hunt for fish. The greed of the cormorant is proverbial. It was ceremonially unclean to the Jews.

Driver in HDB considers 'cormorant' unlikely for shalakh since
the word occurs on both occasions in the middle of a list of owls
(see OWL). He suggests the fisher owl, Ketupa zeylonensis (so
NEB), although this bird is not common in Palestine. NEB follows
Driver in translating ?anaphah as 'cormorant'. See HERON.

[18]

REFERENCES: Lv 11.17; Dt 14.17

DIFFICULT PASSAGES: Is 34.11 (RSV 'hawk') and Zeph 2.14 (RSV 'vulture'). In these passages AV has translated the Hb qaʔath as 'cormorant'. Perhaps the translation 'pelican' (so RV and JB) should be preferred. See PELICAN. NEB has 'horned owl'.

Crane (*Grus grus*)

Crane   Grus grus

Hebrew: 'aghur

DESCRIPTION: The crane is one of the long-legged wading birds. It is dark grey in colour, with a long beak, neck and legs. It breeds in Northern Europe and Asia and goes south during the winter. With a wingspread of 2.4 m, it is the largest bird that flies over Palestine (Parmelee, p 184).

The dictionaries maintain that the meaning of the Hb word is uncertain, and BDB points out that the cry made by a crane does not fit the context of Is 38.14. See OTTP, p 162.

The only certain thing to be said is that the context in Je 8.7 suggests a migratory bird.

In modern Hb 'aghur stands for 'crane'. AV 'swallow' is incorrect. Some prefer to render the Hb as 'wryneck' (Jynx torquilla); see Parmelee (and NEB of Je 8.7). This is a small, shy, migratory bird, about the size of a sparrow. It has a monotonous whistling note which might make it fit Is 38.14.

REFERENCES: Is 38.14; Je 8.7

Deer   Cervus elaphus

Hebrew: ʔayyal,   ʔayyalah (hind), 'opher (young hart, stag)

DESCRIPTION: Bodenheimer enumerates three species of the family cervidae, which were living in ancient Palestine, but have now disappeared. The last specimens were hunted in 1914. They are still to be found in the northern parts of the Middle East. These are tne red deer (Cervus elaphus), the fallow deer (Dama mesopotamica) and the roe deer (Capreolus capreolus). Bodenheimer is inclined to consider ʔayyal as a general name for deer. See FALLOW DEER.

REFERENCES: ʔayyal: Dt 12.15, 22; 14.5; 15.22; 1 K 4.23; Ps 42.1; SS 2.9, 17; 8.14 (NEB 'young wild goat'); Is 35.6; La 1.6 (JB 'ram')
ʔayyalah: Gn 49.21; 2 S 22.34; Job 39.1; Ps 18.33; 22 (title); 29.9; Pr 5.19; SS 2.7; 3.5 (NEB 'goddesses'); Je 14.5
'opher: SS 2.9, 17; 4.5; 7.3; 8.14

DIFFICULT PASSAGES: Gn 49.21: Some understand ʔayyalah seluhah as the roe deer. But most translate 'a swift hind' (cf RSV 'a hind let loose'), with reference to the freedom and frequent movements of the tribe. NEB 'a spreading terebinth'. JB translates ʔayyalah in Ps 29.9 as 'terebinths', and RSV has 'oaks'.

Dog Canis familiaris

Hebrew: <u>kelebh</u>   Greek: <u>kuōn</u>, <u>kunarion</u> (little dog)

DESCRIPTION: In appearance the dog mentioned in the Bible may
have looked like a modern Alsatian, with short pointed ears, a
pointed nose and a long tail. However, we should not think of Biblical dogs as 'the closest friend of man', or a house dog, or a faith-
ful companion. The dog of the Bible is an unclean animal because it
feeds on carrion. It is described as running wild in the village
streets without a master (Ps 59.6). So the stranger arriving at the
village in the evening could find himself surrounded by 'a pack of
dogs' (Ps 22.16-21).

One quality of the dog which was highly esteemed by the Israelites was its watchfulness (Is 56.10). A dumb dog that cannot bark is
like a blind watchman.

The word 'dog' is used figuratively, e. g. as a term of abuse by
Goliath (1 S 17.43). So too, Mephibosheth reveals his humility by
calling himself 'a dead dog' (2 S 9.8). The voracity of the dog, like
that of the pig, made it omnivorous. Dogs served as scavengers in
the village streets, into which the housewives threw all the rubbish
of the house. So it would be no kindness to take bread from the
children and give it to scavenging dogs. It was also customary
among Israelites in the time of Jesus to use the word as a term of
abuse for Gentiles (Mt 15.26; Mk 7.27; and perhaps Mt 7.6), who like
dogs were unclean. <u>Kunarion,</u> as used by Jesus, may have a milder
tone and less rigid meaning: some smaller dogs might be admitted
to the house and show a faith like that of the Canaanite woman in
Mt 15.26.

The word is also used symbolically in Php 3.2 to indicate Juda-
izers and in Rv 22.15 to refer to unclean people in general. In
Dt 23.18 the word refers to a male prostitute.

REFERENCES: kelebh: Ex 11.7; 22.31; Dt 23.18; Jg 7.5; 1 S 17.43;
            <u>24.14</u>; 2 S 3.8; 9.8; 16.9; 1 K 14.11; 16.4; 21.19, 23, 24;
            22.38; 2 K 8.13; 9.10, 36; Job 30.1; Ps 22.16, 20;
            59.6, 14; 68.23; Pr 26.11, 17; Ec 9.4; Is 56.10, 11; 66.3;
            Je 15.3

kuōn and kunarion: Mt 7.6; 15.26, 27; Mk 7.27, 28; Lk 16.21; Php 3.2; 2 P 2.22; Rv 22.15

DIFFICULT PASSAGE: Often the words of Lk 16.21 are understood as a mark of mercy shown to the poor man by dogs, but not by man. It may, however, be interpreted as increasing his sufferings: he is too weak to prevent the touch of an unclean animal, which is scenting a corpse. In that case the words alla kai should indicate an intensification of the poor man's misery.

Dolphin, Dugong   Tursiops truncatus, Dugong dugong

Hebrew: tahash

DESCRIPTION: The Red Sea dugong is an aquatic, herbivorous mammal, belonging to the sirenes. The male has tusk-like upper incisors. It is found in the Red Sea and the Gulf of Aqaba. The bottle-nosed dolphin (Tursiops truncatus) belongs to the dolphins (Delphinidae) and is found in the eastern Mediterranean Sea.

Different translations of the word tahash have been suggested. LXX renders it 'hyacinthine', the Vulgate 'violet-coloured', the Targum 'costly'. Luther and AV have 'badger', which is unlikely in the wilderness of Sinai, though the badger is known in Palestine. Others (Delitzsch quoted in BDB and RSV) have 'goat', which is not improbable for the covering of the tabernacle in the wilderness. RV 'sealskins', JB 'fine leather', NEB 'porpoise-hide' (mg 'sea-cow'). There seems to be no justification for RSV 'sheepskin' in Nu 4.25.

In favour of 'dolphin', the Arabic word for this animal is much like tahash. In favour of 'dugong', travellers have noticed that the Bedouin make sandals from its skin, and this fits with what Ezekiel says (16.10). Here RSV and JB have 'leather', NEB 'stout hide'.

Some commentators leave open the question of the meaning of tahash in Exodus and Numbers. Perhaps the word means simply 'leather' (cf Egyptian ths), but some modern scholars like Noth do not hesitate to identify the leather used for the covering of the tabernacle with the skin of the dugong or dolphin.

REFERENCES: Ex 25.5; 26.14; 35.7, 23; 36.19; 39.34; Nu 4.6, 8, 10-12, 14, 25; Ezk 16.10

Dove Columba livia, Turtur communis

Hebrew: yonah, tor, gozal (young dove)

Greek: peristera

DESCRIPTION: No other birds are mentioned so often in the Bible as doves and pigeons. Pigeons not only lived wild in caves and mountains but were domesticated (Is 60.8). Cheyne in 'The Poly-

Dove (*Turtur communis*)

chrome Edition of the Bible' even translates 'like doves to their cotes'.

According to ancient zoology the dove has no bile; consequently it was considered to be a very peaceful and clean bird, and it became the symbol of Christian virtues (e. g. of gentleness in Mt 10.16). It was used as a sacrifice and sold in the Temple.

As to the Indians of America, so to the Psalmist the dove was a symbol of swiftness (Nida, 'Message and Mission', p 48; Ps 55. 6).

Noah, acting as many mariners have done since his time, observed the flight of the birds (Gn 8). The difference in behavior between the raven and the dove is interesting: the raven, a hardy and sturdy bird, did not return to the ark but overcame the difficulties, whereas the dove 'found no place to set her foot', and so returned to Noah.

NEB translates ṣuṣ in Is 38.14 as 'swallow'. See SWALLOW.

REFERENCES: yonah, tor, gozal: Consult a concordance
    peristera: Mt 3.16; 10.16; 21.12; Mk 1.10; 11.15;
    Lk 2.24; 3.22; Jn 1.32; 2.14, 16
    trugōn: Lk 2.24 (turtledoves - truzō = to coo).

DIFFICULT PASSAGES: 2 K 6.25: The text reads 'dove's dung', as in RSV. Benzinger suggests this may be a designation for some very cheap food (cf JB 'wild onions'). Linnaeus, following an ancient tradition that goes back to the Gk herbalist Dioscorides, believed that the bulbs of Ornithogalum umbellatum, popularly known as Star of Bethlehem, were in fact the 'dove's dung' that was eaten. Josephus (Antiq. 9, IV, 4), mentioning the siege of Samaria, also speaks of 'dove's dung', but without identifying it. It may also be understood not as food, but as fuel (so Dalman). NEB translates as 'locust bean', referring to the carob (q.v.).

Eagle   See VULTURE

Eagle Owl, Long-eared Owl, Bee-Eater   Bubo ascalaphus, Asio otus, Merops apiaster
Hebrew: yanshuph

DESCRIPTION: Most commentators are inclined to identify this bird with a species of larger owls, the Egyptian eagle owl or the ear owl. Driver in HDB suggests screech owl (Strix flammea) (so NEB). The Hb name may be derived either from a root nashaph, meaning 'to blow', as a hint to the sound uttered by the owls, or from a root <u>nesheph,</u> 'twilight', the time when these birds appear.

Both the <u>Bubo ascalaphus</u> and the <u>Asio otus</u> live in caves and among ruins in the regions around Beersheba and the centre of the Edomites, Petra (cf Is 34). See also OSTRICH.

Some (e.g. Noth) translate 'bee-eater', which is a bird of about the size of the thrush, found in Mediterranean countries. It feeds on bees and wasps, has a long beak and is brightly coloured.

The Vulgate translates 'ibis' (see HERON); so does RSV in Lv 11.17, though it retains the 'owl' of AV and RV in Dt 14.16 and Is 34.11.

REFERENCES: Lv 11.17; Dt 14.16; Is 34.11

Eagle owl (*Bubo ascalaphus*)

Fallow deer (*Dama mesopotamica*)

Fallow Deer   Dama mesopotamica

Hebrew: yaḥmur

DESCRIPTION: Some derive the Hb name from a root ḥamar, 'to be red', and thus maintain that the animal must be of a reddish colour.

Modern expositors waver between two possibilities: to identify the yaḥmur with the roe deer (RV, RSV, JB and NEB), or with the fallow deer. It is probably better to follow Bodenheimer and Feliks (in BHH) who identify yaḥmur with the fallow deer. Bodenheimer says that the roe deer does not seem to be mentioned in the Bible.

The fallow deer has rather large horns, and its coat is yellow-brown with spots. It is native to the Mediterranean countries. See also DEER.

REFERENCES: Dt 14.5; 1 K 4.23

Fish piscis, Squalua carcharias

Hebrew: dagh, daghah

Greek: ichthus, ichthudion, enalia (sea creatures), opsarion (lit. 'cooked food'), prosphagion (relish, fish), kētos

DESCRIPTION: The Bible does not mention particular species of fish, but only divides them into clean and unclean (Lv 11.9,10). As most fish in the rivers and lakes of Palestine have fins and scales, few only were placed under prohibition.

The Bible does not mention fishing in the Mediterranean. That this was done is clear, and the name of the city of Sidon (derived from tsudh 'to fish') indicates the fact. It was probably done mostly by the Phoenicians. Fishing in the Sea of Galilee is often mentioned in the New Testament, and the fishermen in this part of Palestine played an important part in the story of Jesus.

Fishes of the Sea of Galilee
(above, *Chromis nilotica;* below, *Labeobarbus canis*)

[27]

Josephus (Bell. Jud. III, book X, 7) describes the Sea of Galilee, mentioning that the water is fresh and clear and good to drink, and that there are many species of fish in this lake which are different from those to be found elsewhere. Present-day zoologists have counted about thirty different species of fish in this lake. The shoals are sometimes unusually large. Fishing was one of the most common occupations in that part of the country, and the towns around the lake were populated with fishermen.

The Sea of Galilee is below the level of the Mediterranean, and is 20 km long and 11 km across at its widest point.

Fishing was done with a hook (Mt 17.27), a cast-net (Mt 4.18) or a drag-net (Mt 13.47). There was no fishing in the Dead Sea because of its high salt content (25 %). This is alluded to in Ezk 47.7-12.

Fishing in the Sea of Galilee was carried out at night. When the water was cool the fish came to the surface and could not see the meshes of the net. This is the background of Simon's protest (Lk 5.5).

Fish was often eaten by the Jews, and no doubt sold at the Fish Gate (2 Ch 33.14). It was eaten boiled, broiled, pickled or smoked (Jn 21.9; Lk 24.42).

REFERENCES: dagh, daghah: Consult a concordance
ichthus: Mt 7.10; 14.17, 19; 15.36; 17.27; Mk 6.38, 41, 43; Lk 5.6, 9; 9.13, 16; 11.11; 24.42; Jn 21.6, 8, 11; 1 Co 15.39
ichthudion: Mt 15.34; Mk 8.7
enalia: Jas 3.7
opsarion: Jn 6.9, 11; 21.9, 10, 13
prosphagion: Jn 21.5
kētos: Mt 12.40

DIFFICULT PASSAGES: Mt 7.10: The comparison between a fish and a serpent may seem strange to many. Perhaps this should be understood in connection with the Law (Lv 11.9, 10) forbidding Jews to eat fish without fins and scales, i.e. serpent-like fish. Another explanation is suggested by the observations of a traveller in

Palestine who noted a large number of snakes swimming in the Sea of Galilee and often biting the hooks of the fishermen. Jesus' meaning, however, is clear: unclean fish or serpents are often caught in the net along with the edible fish, and a man who is not careful may harm those he has no desire to harm. As an earthly father is careful about what he gives his children to eat, so our heavenly Father gives us only what is good for us when we pray.

Jon 1.17; 2.1: The literal translation of dagh gadhol 'a great fish' (as in RSV, JB, NEB) is also justified by the zoologists (according to Bodenheimer). The old idea of this monster being a whale (which is a mammal) is unlikely, since the gullet of the whale is too narrow to allow it to swallow a man. Also, whales are rare in the Mediterranean. The 'great fish' is likely to have been a big shark, squalua carcharias glaucus, 6 to 7 m long, which is known to have swallowed men whole. Cf kētos (Mt 12.40), a big fish, sea monster; so NEB, JB, but RSV has 'whale'.

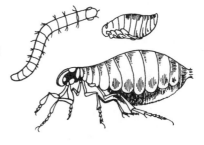

Flea (*Pulex irritans*)

Flea   Pulex irritans

Hebrew: par'osh

DESCRIPTION: A description of the flea will be unnecessary in this connection. It is sufficient to notice that David refers to a flea as a very small and insignificant creature, thus stressing the difference in status between King Saul and himself (1 S 24.14).

REFERENCES: 1 S 24.14; 26.20 (Masoretic text)

DIFFICULT PASSAGE: 1 S 26.20: The Masoretic text has 'the king of Israel came out to look for a flea' (par'osh ehadh) (NEB). RSV and JB follow the Septuagint reading 'has come out to seek my soul' (naphshi, i.e. my life), which is undoubtedly the better, because the Masoretic text may be an echo of 24.14 (thus Hertzberg and Budde).

Fly   Musca

Hebrew: zebhubh

DESCRIPTION: zebhubh is a general word for 'fly' without statement as to the species. Musca vicina is the housefly. The two
passages in which the fly is mentioned both prove what a nuisance
and danger it is to the inhabitants of warm countries. Pliny's
Natural History (10.28) says that the people of antiquity believed
flies to be carriers of plague, and feared them accordingly.

Disagreement still prevails as to the origin and meaning of the
name of the god of Ekron (2 K 1). Some read Ba'al zebhubh, 'the
lord of flies', indicating the extent to which flies were feared, so
that a god was worshipped in the hope that he might avert the plague
from the people. Others maintain it to be a mistake for Ba'al zebhul
(as in Mt 10.25). zebhul is then derived from a similar word in Uga-
ritic meaning 'high, sublime'. JB explains Ba'al zebhubh as a
'mocking pun on the god's real name, Baalzebul'.

REFERENCES: Ec 10.1; Is 7.18 (JB 'mosquito')

Fly (*Musca*)

Foxes (left, *Vulpes nilotica;* right, *Canis aureus*)

Fox, Jackal   Vulpes nilotica, V. flavescens, Canis aureus

Hebrew: shu'al, tan, ʔi   Greek: alōpēx

DESCRIPTION: It seems clear that the OT sometimes uses the
word shu'al for the jackal (Canis aureus) as well as the fox (Vulpes
nilotica, flavescens), although the Hebrews had two other names for
this animal (tan, ʔi).   The fox and the jackal are very much alike,
except that the jackal has a broader head, shorter nose and ears,
and longer legs.   The similarity between the two accounts for their
not always being distinguished.   In the OT, therefore, the context must
decide, where possible, how the word shu'al should be translated.

One difference in habit may be decisive: the fox is a solitary
creature, whereas the jackal is gregarious.   Jackals stay together
in packs and hide during the day in some cave, where they can be
caught.   It may therefore be more correct to translate 'three hundred jackals' in Jg 15.4 (as does NEB).

[31]

Another difference is that the jackal feeds on carrion, which the fox does not. Ps 63.10 may, therefore, more correctly be rendered 'prey for jackals', as in RSV, JB and NEB.

Although the word 'fox' in the Talmud and Midrash is often used to characterize an insignificant person (as opposed to a 'lion', who is a great man), it is evident that in Nehemiah and the Song of Solomon 'fox' is used symbolically of the enemies of God and his people, those who tear down and undermine in a cunning way. However, 'jackal' would fit equally well here.

In Lk 13 the word alōpēx is used metaphorically of a cunning and crafty man. It indicates that Jesus had seen through the plans of the tetrarch. 'Fox' is more appropriate here.

REFERENCES: shu'al: Jg 15.4; Ne 4.3; Ps 63.10; SS 2.15; La 5.18; Ezk 13.4

tan: Job 30.29; Ps 44.19; Is 13.22; 34.13; 35.7; 43.20; Je 9.11; 10.22; 14.6; 49.33; 51.37; Ezk 29.3; Mi 1.8; Mal 1.3

ʔi: Is 13.22; 34.14 (RSV 'hyena'); Je 50.39

alōpēx: Mt 8.20; Lk 9.58; 13.32

Frog (*Rana punctata*)

[32]

Frog   Rana punctata

Hebrew: tsephardea'   Greek: batrachos

DESCRIPTION: The frog is an amphibious animal and is mentioned
in two connections in the Bible: in the second Egyptian plague, and
in the vision of Rv 16.13.   Frog plagues are said to be not uncommon
in Egypt, but the intensity described in the book of Exodus is unusual,
and the fact that the plague started and stopped on the command of
God makes it a miracle. The frog in question is probably Rana
punctata, the spotted frog of Egypt.

The vision of Rv 16 is evidently an allusion to the Egyptian
plague. Its symbolic character points to the fact that the frog in
Persian religion belongs to the creatures of Ahriman, the wicked
god. The frog is a symbol of uncleanness, a demon.

REFERENCES: tsephardea': Ex 8.2-9, 11-13; Ps 78.45; 105.30
                     batrachos: Rv 16.13

Gadfly

Hebrew: qerets

DESCRIPTION: a cattle-biting fly. AV 'destruction'.

REFERENCE: Je 46.20

Gazelle Gazella dorcas, Gazella arabica

Hebrew: tsebhi, tsebhiyyah

DESCRIPTION: The Hb word means 'beauty', but is also the name
of a graceful and beautiful animal. Most authorities today identify
this animal with the gazelle, i. e. Gazella dorcas or Gazella arabica.
It is smaller than the antelope, about 1 m long and 53 cm high. The
high colour of the fur is yellowish brown (dorcas) or grey (arabica).

[33]

It is native to the Middle East where it lives in small herds or alone. Its only means of defence are its colour and the speed with which it can escape. The horns carried by both sexes are not used as a weapon.

REFERENCES: tsebhi: Dt 12.15, 22; 14.5; 15.22; 2 S 2.18; 1 K 4.23;
                          1 Ch 12.8; Pr 6.5; SS 2.7, 9, 17; 3.5; 8.14; Is 13.14
                 tsebhiyyah: SS 4.5; 7.3

Gazelle (*Gazella dorcas*)

Gecko Hemidactylus turcicus

Hebrew: ?anaqah

DESCRIPTION: Luther rendered the Hb word as 'hedgehog', but according to the Mishnah the skin of the animal mentioned in Lv 11.30 was delicate, which can scarcely be said of a hedgehog.

Modern translators have connected the animal's name with the identical Hb noun denoting 'crying', a plaintive sound often heard from geckoes.

In Lv 11 the gecko is listed among the unclean animals, whereas the Mishnah (according to Feliks in BHH) says its meat is fit for eating.

The gecko is a well-known denizen of houses in Palestine. It is a wall-lizard, which runs over walls and ceilings by means of the suction provided by sucking-discs on its toes. It lives on mosquitoes, flies and spiders. NEB translates leṭa?ah as 'wall-gecko' and koaḥ as 'sand-gecko'. See also LIZARD and CHAMELEON.

REFERENCE: Lv 11.30

Gecko (*Hemidactylus turcicus*)

Gnat, Mosquito   culex

Hebrew: kinnam, kinnim   Greek: kōnōps

DESCRIPTION: Various species of gnats and mosquitoes are found in the Middle East. Their bite is almost always extremely irritating, and four species of mosquito are fever-carriers. The practice of straining liquids referred to in Mt 23.24 is based on regulations in Lv 11.32f.

The third of the Egyptian plagues may have been of mosquitoes. Herodotus also (II.95) gives a vivid description of Egyptian gnats.

He says they are innumerable, and that people try to avoid them by climbing high towers to sleep during the night, or by covering their beds with a fishing net.

Bodenheimer, however, in ID states that the Hebrew words ken, kinnam, kinnim refer to lice, Pediculus humanus, the human body louse. There is little doubt, he says, that the third Egyptian plague refers to this insect, as it was held in great abomination in Egypt. Josephus also (Antiquitates Judaicæ Book II, 14, 3) identifies this plague with an attack of lice. NEB has 'maggots'.

REFERENCES: kinnam, kinnim: Ex 8.16, 17, 18; Ps 105.31; Is 51.6
kōnōps: Mt 23.24

DIFFICULT PASSAGES: Is 51.6 has the Hb word ken, 'in the same manner' or 'like this'. The first of these translations would point backwards to the 'wearing out of a garment' and 'the vanishing of smoke', which is inadequate in connection with the verb 'die'. The second has been adopted by some who imply a gesture meaning 'like nothing', perhaps a snap of the fingers. Some consider ken to be a collective noun to be translated 'a swarm of mosquitoes'. It is better to read kinnam or kinnim, 'gnats'. So RSV and RV mg. JB has 'vermin'.

Mt 23.24: the translation 'gnat' for kōnōps is most likely. NEB has 'midge'. AG mentions the possibility that the word may refer to a certain worm found in wine.

Goat, Buck, Kid Capra hircus mambrica

Hebrew: 'ez, seh, sa'ir, tayish, 'attudh, tsaphir, zemer (wild goat), se'irah, gedhi

Greek: eriphos, eriphion (kid, he-goat), tragos, aigeios (of a goat)

DESCRIPTION: The goat belongs to the family of the hollow-horned ruminants. A detailed description is unnecessary. Black was probably the prevailing colour of Palestinian goats (SS 1.5; 4.1; 6.5), and

Goat (*Capra hircus mambrica*)

'speckled and spotted goats' were a rarity; that is why Jacob's request sounds very modest (Gn 30.32). However, there may have been red goats. (See 1 S 19.13 [if David was red-haired and not 'ruddy', 1 S 16.12] and Gn 27.16, where Jacob makes up so as to resemble his red, hairy brother.)

Goat hair was not considered to be as useful or valuable as wool. This, as well as the fact that the buck is wilder than the ram, may be relevant in connection with the separation of the goats from the sheep (Mt 25.32f).

The Syrian goat is characterized by its long pendulous ears and backward-curving horns. As a sacrifice the goat was used 'from the eighth day on' (Lv 22.27). The scapegoat is mentioned in Lv 16.9.

REFERENCES: tahash (RSV 'goat'): see DOLPHIN
'ez, seh, sa'ir: Consult a concordance
tayish: Gn 30.35; 32.14; 2 Ch 17.11; Pr 30.31
'attudh: Consult a concordance
tsaphir: 2 Ch 29.21; Ezra 8.35; Dn 8.5, 8, 21
zemer: Dt 14.5
se'irah: Lv 4.28; 5.6
gedhi: Consult a concordance
eriphos: Mt 25.32; Lk 15.29
eriphion: Mt 25.33 (Lk 15.29 in Codex B)
tragos: He 9.12, 13, 19; 10.4
aigeios: He 11.37

DIFFICULT PASSAGES: It should be noted that the OT does not
always distinguish between 'sheep' and 'goat'. The Hb word seh
therefore may sometimes be translated 'lamb'. The translation of
zemer is uncertain: RSV and JB 'mountain sheep', NEB 'rock-goat'.
Ed. König, 'Bergziege'. Kautzsch believes it to be a kind of antelope. 'attudh may in some connections mean 'leader'. sa'ir in
Gn 27.11 means 'hairy'; in Lv 17.7; 2 Ch 11.15; Is 13.21; 34.14 RSV and
JB translate 'satyr'; others explain it as a kind of demon in the shape
of a goat.

Goose (*Branta ruficullis*)

Goose Branta

Hebrew: barburim

DESCRIPTION: The Hb words in 1 K 4.23, barburim ʔabhusim, literally mean some kind of fattened fowl (as in RSV, NEB).   As the Hb bar means 'pure white', some commentators have suggested the swan, as a clean, white bird.   But Bodenheimer says that no swan is common in Palestine.   On the other hand, ivory carvings from Megiddo which date from the tenth century BC represent peasants carrying geese to market, and the oldest Egyptian paintings of birds (from the tomb of Ra-hotep at Meidum) show different kinds of geese feeding on the ground (cf Parmelee, p 82).   Several translators are therefore inclined to identify the barburim with 'geese'.   The species cannot be decided.

Other suggestions have been made, such as the guinea hen and the lark-heeled cuckoo (Centropus ægypticus Shelley), which when stuffed was considered a great delicacy in ancient Greece; JB translates 'cuckoo'.   The Arabic name for chicken, birbir, may have been derived from barburim.

REFERENCE: 1 K 4.23

Hare Lepus syriacus

Hebrew: ʔarnebheth

DESCRIPTION: The hare is listed in the Law among the unclean animals on the ground that 'it chews the cud, but does not part the hoof'.

It is generally assumed that the Hebrews thought the hare was a ruminant through observing the peculiar movements of its jaws when chewing.   Today we know that physiologically the hare is a rodent, although the zoologists Olsen and Madsen (Investigations on pseudo-rumination in rabbits, 1943) have demonstrated that the hare and the rabbit perform a kind of rumination.

[39]

There are four species of hare in Palestine. [6]The most common is the Lepus syriacus which is 60 cm shorter than the European and has shorter ears.

REFERENCES: Lv 11.6; Dt 14.7

Hare (*Lepus syriacus*)

Hawk, Buzzard, Falcon, Harrier, Kite   Accipiter nisus, Buteo ferox, Falco peregrinus, Circus spp., Milvus migrans

Hebrew: nets, ?ayyah, dayyah, da?ah

DESCRIPTION: In modern Hb nets is the name of the sparrow-hawk. One cannot, however, assume that Biblical writers or modern translators distinguish accurately between the various species. Driver in HDB suggests the following identifications:

nets: kestrel (Falco tinnunculus) and/or sparrow-hawk (Accipiter nisus). RSV, JB and NEB all have 'hawk'.
?ayyah: falcon (Falco peregrinus), but may well include the buzzard (Buteo ferox) or harrier (Circus spp.). NEB has 'falcon', JB 'buzzard', RSV 'falcon' in Lv but 'kite' in Dt.
ra?ah, da?ah, dayyah: kite (Milvus migrans). So JB and NEB, and RSV in Lv, but 'buzzard' in Dt.

REFERENCES: <u>nets</u>: Lv 11.16; Dt 14.15; Job 39.26
<u>ʔayyah</u>: Lv 11.14; Dt 14.13; Job 28.7
<u>dayyah</u>: Dt 14.13; Is 34.15
<u>daʔah</u>: Lv 11.14 (? Dt 14.13)

DIFFICULT PASSAGES: Dt 14.13: The words <u>raʔah</u> and <u>dayyah</u> are probably both scribal errors for <u>daʔah</u>, 'vulture' (q.v.) or 'kite'.

RSV translates <u>qaʔath</u> as 'hawk' in Is 34.11. But see PELICAN.

Heron <u>Ardea</u>

Hebrew: <u>ʔanaphah</u>

DESCRIPTION: In modern Hb this is the name for the heron family, and in Biblical times also it may have been a generic name, covering the seven species of this family living in Palestine.

The heron belongs to the waders. It is a large bird with a long bill and neck, and long legs suitable for wading in shallow waters where it probes in the mud for fish and small reptiles.

Among the species living in Palestine the most common is the buff-backed heron or white ibis (<u>Ardea bubulcus</u>). It lives predominantly on Lake Huleh in the north. The common heron (<u>Ardea cinerea</u>) and the purple heron (<u>Ardea purpurea</u>) live near the river Jordan and on the coast.

Driver in HDB suggests that <u>ʔanaphah</u> may be the cormorant (so NEB). There seems to be no justification for RSV's translation of <u>yanshuph</u> as 'ibis' in Lv 11.17. See EAGLE OWL.

REFERENCES: Lv 11.19; Dt 14.18

DIFFICULT PASSAGE: For Job 39.13, see OTTP, p 90.

[41]

Hoopoe (*Upupa epops*)

Hoopoe Upupa

Hebrew: dukhiphath

DESCRIPTION: The hoopoe comes to Palestine in spring each year. It is conspicuous for its plumage, tall crest and odd movements. It was judged unclean as it finds its food on dunghills and does not clear its nest of filth. The flesh, though tasty to eat, has a bad smell.

RV, RSV, JB and NEB, with LXX and Vulgate, translate 'hoopoe'. AV 'lapwing'.

REFERENCES: Lv 11.19; Dt 14.18

Hornet Vespa orientalis

Hebrew: tsir'ah

DESCRIPTION: In modern Hb the word is used for wasps in general (Vespidæ), but is commonly rendered 'hornet' in Bible translations. In all three references the hornet stands as a symbol of military force. (For illustration see page 10.)

Some modern expositors (KB, Noth) prefer to render the word 'depression' or 'discouragement', comparing the Hb with an Arabic verb dara'a which means 'to subject oneself, to debase oneself'. Cf NEB 'panic'.

REFERENCES: Ex 23.28; Dt 7.20; Jos 24.12

Horse Equus caballus

Hebrew: ṣuṣ, parash, rekhesh, ʔabbir (literally: 'strong, valiant')

Greek: hippos

DESCRIPTION: The steppes of Central Asia are considered to be the original habitat of the horse, and in these open spaces its special qualities have developed. From Central Asia the breeding of horses spread towards the south and west.

Bodenheimer mentions the horse among the mammals from the Palæolithicum of the Mount Carmel caves (p 27). The earliest evidence for the use of war chariots drawn by horses dates from the time of the Hyksos tribes, who between 1800 and 1600 BC subjugated parts of Mesopotamia, Syria and Egypt.

According to the Bible, the horse was not domesticated by the Jews until the days of King Solomon. Horses mentioned in the Pentateuch are Egyptian, or come from neighbouring countries. Canaanite war chariots are mentioned in Jos 17.16 and Jg 5.22. According to Dt 17.16, keeping horses was considered by the Israelites to be a sign of impiety. This is why Joshua (11.9) and later David (2 S 8.4) hamstrung all captured horses. They led their armies on foot (Ps 18.36) and not mounted on horseback.

[43]

Horse (*Equus caballus*)

A great change in the cultural life of Israel came with King Solomon, who imported horses from Egypt and Cilicia (1 K 10.28), predominantly for military purposes. 'To rely on horses' or 'go to Egypt for help' (Is 31.1) therefore indicates trust in material resources and not in God.

The horse was the mount of the warrior, and by entering Jerusalem on an ass Jesus indicated that he was coming as the Prince of peace.

Colours play an important part in the book of Revelation, and the different colours of the four horses have a symbolic meaning: white, fiery red, black and pale mean respectively victory, violence, famine and death.

REFERENCES: ṣuṣ: Consult a concordance
parash: 1 S 8.11; 1 K 4.26; Is 21.7, 9; 28.28;
   Ezk 27.14; Joel 2.4; Na 3.3; Hbk 1.8
rekhesh: 1 K 4.28; Es 8.10, 14; Mi 1.13
ʔabbir: may stand for 'horse' in: Jg 5.22; Je 8.16;
   47.3; 50.11
hippos: Jas 3.3; Rv 6.2, 4, 5, 8; 9.7, 9, 17, 19; 14.20;
   18.13; 19.11, 14, 18, 19, 21

DIFFICULT PASSAGES: The Hb word parash is used both for 'horse' and 'horseman', and not even the context will always make clear which is meant.

ʔabbir stands for 'horse' in the above references according to most translators.

Hyena Hyaena striata

Hebrew: tsebho'im, tsabhua' (tsiy)

DESCRIPTION: The striped hyena, a carrion-eater which only appears at night, is quite common in Palestine and may have been

Hyena (*Hyæna striata*)

so in OT times. Some say that the only evidence for the existence of the hyena at that time is a geographical name 'the valley of the hyenas', the valley of tsebho'im, 1 S 13.18. Others find this animal mentioned also in Je 12.9 (so NEB). See OTTP, p 165. It is very likely that the word tsabhua' should be translated 'hyena' (thus Feliks in BHH, Davidson, Lisowsky).

The Hb word tsiy means either a desert dweller or a creature that howls or yelps, that is to say some wild animal, which is identified by some translators with the hyena or the wild cat. Others translate 'demon'.

RSV translates ?i as 'hyena' in two places. See FOX.

REFERENCES: tsabhua': Je 12.9
            tsebho'im: 1 S 13.18; Ne 11.34
            tsiy: Ps 72.9; 74.14; Is 13.21; 23.13; 34.14; Je 50.39

Ibex Capra ibex nubiana, Capra beden

Hebrew: ya'el, ya'alah

DESCRIPTION: The ibex, a type of wild goat, is still found in Southern Palestine, Sinai, Egypt and Arabia; it was known also in ancient times, as is evident from rock carvings. However, it is often difficult in these monuments to distinguish the ibex from the Capra hircus, the true wild goat. The rump of the ibex is more compact and the horns slender and curved back. All translations render 'wild goat'.

REFERENCES: 1 S 24.2; Job 39.1; Ps 104.18; Pr 5.19

DIFFICULT PASSAGES: In 1 S 24.2 tsure hayye'elim may well be a proper name for a precipice (see RSV, 'Wildgoats' Rocks').

Dt 14.5: RSV translates dishon as 'ibex', but it is better to identify this with the antelope.

?aqqo in the same verse is rendered 'ibex' by JB, but 'wild goat' by RSV and NEB; te?o is 'antelope' in RSV and NEB. But the

Ibex (*Capra ibex nubiana*)

identification of these two Hb words is very doubtful. Traditionally te?o is 'wild ox'. Tristram identifies it with the oryx (as in JB), described under ANTELOPE.

Leech   Hirudinea

Hebrew: 'aluqah

DESCRIPTION: According to Bodenheimer (p 76f), leeches have served for cupping blood in many different diseases at least since 63 BC. They were used instead of cupping glasses, and when satiated they dropped off by the weight of the blood sucked, or were forced to do so when salt was sprinkled on them.

The local giant species of Hirudinea is Limnatis nilotica.

'aluqah may be derived from a root which corresponds to the Arabic root meaning 'to adhere'; or it may be an Aramaic loan word. Some modern commentators consider the word to be a proper name, not to be translated. Or they conceive it to be a vampire-like demon (RV mg). ID states that there is no dispute over the interpretation of 'aluqah as 'leech'.

REFERENCE: Pr 30.15

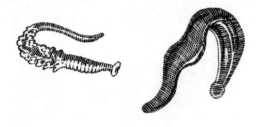

Leech (*Limnatis nilotica*)

Leopard   Felis pardus

Hebrew: namer   Greek: pardalis

DESCRIPTION: The leopard is one of the most dangerous beasts of prey, dangerous not only to domestic animals, but also to man. Its movements are very graceful. Its fur is yellow on the back and sides, with black spots grouped in patterns. These colours make it easy for the animal to hide on the forest floor with its changing light and shadow.

The leopard was common in Palestine in OT times and is still found there occasionally. Two place names suggest leopards' haunts: Nu 32.36 'Beth-nimrah' (leopards' house), and Is 15.6 and Je 48.34 'the waters of Nimrim'. 'The mountains of leopards' (SS 4. 8) may be regarded as a place name or a poetical term.

The lurking of the leopard, the suddenness of its unexpected attack, and its noiseless movements symbolize God's wrath (Ho 13.7).

The savagery of the leopard is proverbial. Isaiah can find no better illustration of the kingdom of peace than the leopard lying down with the kid (Is 11.6).

Leopard (*Felis pardus*)

REFERENCES: namer: SS 4.8; Is 11.6; Je 5.6; 13.23; Ho 13.7;
                 Hbk 1.8
             nemar (Aramaic): Dn 7.6
             pardalis: Rv 13.2

DIFFICULT PASSAGES: Some commentators prefer to translate
namer in Hbk 1.8 as 'cheetah' (so NEB) or 'hunting leopard' after
Tristram, because the cheetah was used for hunting in the past.

   As the tiger has never lived in Palestine, the word ḥabharburoth
in Je 13.23 should be translated 'spots' and not 'stripes'. The tiger
has stripes, the leopard spots.

Lion Felis leo (persicus), Panthera leo (persica)

Hebrew: ʔari, ʔaryeh, lebhi, labhiʔ, layish, shaḥal
       plural: bene labhi, gor, gur (young lions), kephir

Greek: leōn

DESCRIPTION: Bodenheimer says that in ancient times the terri-
tories of the African and Persian lions met in the Middle East, and
that up to the 19th century the Persian lion was still found in Iraq.

The lion is one of the largest and strongest carnivores, dangerous not only to domestic cattle, but also to man (1 K 13.24; 20.36;
2 K 17.25). Its majestic appearance is heightened by its swift movements and fearlessness, and also by its mane. Thus it has become
a proverbial symbol of majesty and strength. See Jg 14.18.

Lions are usually found in pairs, though sometimes in large
numbers. The lion's lair is a hollow in the ground, hidden behind
shrubbery. In Palestine they seem to prefer the sub-tropical vegetation of the Jordan valley ('the jungle of the Jordan', Je 49.19). The
lion lies in wait for its prey, killing smaller animals by a blow of
the paw, larger ones by a bite in the throat. It does not stay in the
same place more than a couple of days. But the big forests of
Lebanon seem to have had 'dens of lions' in Biblical times (SS 4.8),
and the Bible also mentions the Negeb, the desert-like country in
the south of Palestine, as their home (Is 30.6).

It should be noted that the lion is used by the Bible as a symbol
of strength in a good as well as in a bad sense: 'the lion of the tribe
of Judah' (Rv 5.5), the cruelty of enemies (Je 51.38), and the supreme
enemy, the Devil (1 P 5.8).

For an effective and impressive description of the peace of the
messianic kingdom, see Is 11.6, 7: 'the lion shall eat straw like the
ox'.

REFERENCES: ʔari and ʔaryeh: Consult a concordance
                lebhi, labhiʔ: Gn 49.9; Nu 23.24; 24.9; Dt 33.20;
                Job 4.11; 38.39; Ps 57.4; Is 5.29; 30.6; Ho 13.8;
                Joel 1.6; Na 2.11, 12

layish: Job 4.11; Pr 30.30; Is 30.6
shaḥal: Job 4.10; 10.16; 28.8; Ps 91.13; Pr 26.13;
  Ho 5.14; 13.7
gor and gur: Gn 49.9; Dt 33.22; Je 51.38; La 4.3;
  Ezk 19.2, 3, 5; Na 2.11, 12
kephir: Consult a concordance
leōn: 2 Ti 4.17; He 11.33; 1 P 5.8; Rv 4.7; 5.5; 9.8, 17;
  10.3; 13.2

DIFFICULT PASSAGES: Is 21.8: see OTTP, p 143.

Is 30.6: see OTTP, p 145. The meaning of the Hb word mehem
is not clear, so some commentators (e. g. Procksch) make a conjecture and read nohem, 'growling' or 'roaring'. It is translated in
this way by Dhorme, Cheyne, Kautzsch, JB and NEB.

La 4.3: gur here should be translated 'a young jackal' (as RSV,
JB) and not 'the whelp of a lion'. NEB has 'whales'.

Ezk 38.13: As the 'young lions' have nothing to do with the
'merchants of Tarshish', some commentators read instead of
kephireyha, rokeleyha or kena'aneyha, 'their tradesmen' (so NEB).
The LXX reads kōmai from Hb kephareyha, 'its villages', and this is
followed by the RSV.

Job 28.8 shaḥats may be translated 'lion' or 'a proudly walking
animal' (cf RSV and NEB 'proud beasts').

Little Owl   Athene noctua glaux

Hebrew: koṣ

DESCRIPTION: The Hb word koṣ is today used for the little owl,
Athene noctua, as in Dt 14.16 (RSV). Driver in HDB considers it may
well be the tawny owl, Strix aluco (so NEB). NEB translates tinshemeth in Lv 11.18 and Dt 14.16 as 'little owl'. See CHAMELEON.

The little owl is the smallest among the nocturnal birds of prey.
It is to be found everywhere in Palestine in lonely places among ruins
and tombs, in rocks and thickets. The psalmist (Ps 102) mentions

the owl because he feels himself a 'desolate mourner amidst ruins in the desert' (Wellhausen), cf vv 14 and 16 with v 6.

Owls feed on mice and serpents, swallowing the prey whole and afterwards vomiting the indigestible parts such as bones and fur.

REFERENCES: Lv 11.17; Dt 14.16; Ps 102.6

Lizard   Lacerta

Hebrew: leṭaʔah

DESCRIPTION: This Hb word which only occurs in Lv 11.30 is translated 'lizard' in RSV. While Gesenius and BDB render 'a kind of lizard', KB 'gecko', Bodenheimer is inclined to understand the Hb as a common name for lizards. NEB 'wall-gecko'. JB transliterates.

Lizards abound in warm countries, and a traveller once counted 44 different species in Palestine; at any rate the number is very great.

Besides the Lacertidæ, some of the other families represented in Palestine are the Scincidæ, Zonuridæ, Agamidæ and Monitoridæ. The 'sand lizard', with which RSV identifies the Hb word homeṭ (Lv 11.30), is a skink, a member of the Scincidæ. It is chiefly to be found in desert places, where its yellowish colour is protective. Unlike the true lizard it does not climb, but hides under stones or in holes. NEB 'great lizard', JB 'chameleon'.

RSV renders koaḥ (Lv 11.30) by 'land crocodile'. This is better known under the name 'land monitor', and belongs to the family of Monitoridæ or Varanidæ. It lives in the deserts of S. Palestine, Sinai and Egypt. It is up to 1.5 m long, with a long snout and sharp teeth. NEB 'sand-gecko', JB transliterates.

On the whole we are inclined to follow Bodenheimer in his opinion that the reptiles mentioned in Lv 11.30 are all unidentifiable. See also GECKO and CHAMELEON. For semamith in Pr 30.28, see SPIDER.

REFERENCE: Lv 11.30

Locust, Grasshopper   Oedipoda migratoria, Locusta viridissima

Hebrew: ?arbeh, gebh (only in plural: gebhim), gobhay, gazam, haghabh, hasil, hargol, yeleq, sol'am, tselatsal

Greek: akris

DESCRIPTION: The migratory locust, to which probably most of the passages refer, belongs to the order of Orthoptera which is divided into forty or more species. It has six legs and four wings. The grasshopper or Locusta viridissima belongs to the Acridiidae family.

The locust is well known in Palestine and Egypt and the Bible gives some vivid descriptions of its habits, especially in 'the plague of locusts' in Ex 10 and the book of Joel. Some of the Hb words which the translators render 'locust' or 'grasshopper' are derived from roots meaning 'to devour' (gazam) or 'to swallow' (sol'am), thus describing the main characteristic of the insect; cf also tselatsal, a whirring insect. The OT references give an idea of how disastrous the attack of a locust swarm might be to the country, and therefore it is often a symbol of God's destroying judgment. The numerous Hb words which are translated 'grasshopper', 'locust' or 'cricket' may indicate different species but may also mean the locust in different stages of development. It must be admitted that the different species cannot be identified by means of the Hb words, e. g. in Lv 11 and Joel 1.

Am 7.1-2 gives an indication of the stages of locust development. Harvest begins in Palestine in April, and in this month the locust is at the nymph stage and more voracious than at any other time. Locusts have three stages: caterpillar, nymph and mature. The nymph has small wings, but cannot yet fly.

REFERENCES: ?arbeh: Consult a concordance
             gebh: Is 33.4
             gobhay: Am 7.1; Na 3.17
             gazam: Joel 1.4; 2.25; Am 4.9
             haghabh: Lv 11.22; Nu 13.33; 2 Ch 7.13; Ec 12.5;
               Is 40.22

[53]

hasil: 1 K 8.37; 2 Ch 6.28; Ps 78.46; Is 33.4;
  Joel 1.4; 2.25
hargol: Lv 11.22
yeleq: Ps 105.34; Je 51.14, 27; Joel 1.4; 2.25;
  Na 3.15, 16
sol'am: Lv 11.22
tselatsal: Dt 28.42; Is 18.1
akris: Mt 3.4; Mk 1.6; Rv 9.3, 7

DIFFICULT PASSAGES: In Na 3.17 keghobh gobhay is perhaps a dittography and should read keghobhay, but it does not affect the meaning.

Ec 12.5 has been interpreted in different ways. RSV 'the grasshopper drags itself along' is probably right, because the word haghabh may indicate the nymph or caterpillar, which creeps but cannot fly. JB 'The grasshopper is heavy with food', NEB 'the locust's paunch is swollen'.

Is 18.1 tsiltsal: the root ts-l-ts-l means 'to tingle, quiver'. tseltselim 'cymbals', tselatsal 'whirring insect'. RSV and JB 'land of whirring wings' may be followed. LXX renders 'ships, boats' (so NEB).

akris in Matthew and Mark is sometimes rendered 'carob pods'. But the eating of locusts is nothing unusual among desert tribes.

Mole Spalax ehrenbergi

Hebrew: hapharparah

DESCRIPTION: The Syrian mole rat belongs to the rodents, and is quite common in Palestine. It has some resemblance to the European mole; it is grey in colour, but is larger, reaching a length of 20 cm, and it does not belong to the same order. It lives underground and feeds on vegetables, especially bulbs.

The Masoretic text in Is 2.20 has haphor peroth, but it is better to read with one Greek version haparparoth, the plural of hapharparah, 'moles'. NEB 'dung-beetles'.

Mole (*Spalax ehrenbergi*)

REFERENCE: Is 2.20

DIFFICULT PASSAGES: Lv 11.29: ḥoledh is translated 'mole' in Gesenius and JB, but the European talpa does not live in Palestine. NEB 'mole-rat'. BDB and Bertholet translate 'weasel', as do AV and RSV; this is probably more correct.

Lv 11.30 tinshemeth is only transliterated in some versions. Others translate 'mole rat', but most identify it with the chameleon (q.v.).

Moth   Tineola pellionella

Hebrew: 'ash, ṣaṣ   Greek: sēs

DESCRIPTION: Tineidæ is a family belonging to the order Lepidoptera, which includes moths and butterflies. Only one of these species is referred to in the Bible, namely, that which is known for its ability to damage woollen clothes. The Israelites did not know that the harm is done not by the full-grown insect, but by its larva

[55]

Moths (*Tineola pellionella*)

which eats the woollen material, into which the eggs are placed by the female insect.

REFERENCES: 'ash: Job 4.19; 13.28; 27.18; Ps 39.11; Is 50.9; 51.8;
Ho 5.12

şaş: Is 51.8

sēs: Mt 6.19, 20; Lk 12.33; Jas 5.2 (sētobrōtos:
moth-eaten)

DIFFICULT PASSAGES: Job 27.18: RSV reads 'the house which he builds is like a spider's web', following the Greek and Syriac versions (JB similar). Weiser translates 'He has built his house like a moth', saying that this simile of a 'moth's nest' expresses the rapid destruction of worldly foundations, which overnight changes a rich man into a beggar. NEB translates 'bird's nest' here and in Job 4.19.

Is 51.8b: RV and RSV translate the word sas as 'worm', and it is appropriate to take this as the larva of the moth.

Mouse Muridæ

Hebrew: 'akhbar

DESCRIPTION: The Hb word 'akhbar is a collective name for all smaller rodents of the family muridæ; a closer identification of the species is more doubtful. In our time more than twenty different species of smaller rodents have been found in Palestine.

1 S 6 probably refers to the Levant vole (Microtus guentheri), as it eats up the crops in the fields (JB and NEB 'rats'). Some commentators think the story in 1 S 5 and 6 suggests that the mice might also have caused the tumours. Bodenheimer does not see any connection between the epidemic and the voles. Others understand by the story that the gifts of gold offered by the Philistines were shaped as tumours and of the size of a mouse.

The Jews were forbidden to eat mice (Lv 11 and Is 66.17: JB 'rat', NEB 'jerboa').

REFERENCES: Lv 11.29; 1 S 6.4, 5, 11, 18; Is 66.17

DIFFICULT PASSAGE: Je 5.26: see OTTP, p 160. It may be added that Bodenheimer regards shakh as a word for mice — here used as a verb.

Mule Equus asinus mulus, mula

Hebrew: peredh (m) pirdah (f)

DESCRIPTION: The mule is a hybrid between a mare and a male ass. Mules were not bred in the land of Israel as cross-breeding was prohibited in the Law of Moses (Lv 19.19). Consequently they must have been imported from the time of King David when they are first mentioned in the Bible. Ezekiel 27.14 reports the importation of mules to Tyre from Togarmah.

The mule was (and is) valued highly for riding and for carrying heavy burdens, especially in warm mountain regions.

REFERENCES: <u>peredh:</u> Consult a concordance
<u>pirdah:</u> 1 K 1.33, 38, 44

DIFFICULT PASSAGES: Gn 36.24 has a word of dubious meaning: <u>yemim</u>. AV and NEB translate 'mules'; RV, RSV and JB follow Vulgate in translating 'hot springs'. Some commentators propose to alter the Hebrew to <u>mayim,</u> 'water'.

Es 8.10, 14: AV translates the Hb <u>rekhesh</u> 'mules'. RV, RSV, JB and NEB more correctly '(swift) horses'.

Mule (*Equus asinus mulus*)

Night-Hag Strix flammea (?)

Hebrew: lilith

DESCRIPTION: AV translates 'screech owl', RSV 'night hag'.
There is no unanimity as to the rendering of lilith. Some authorities
(like ID) translate 'owl', others (like Feliks) explain it as a night-
demon. Driver in HDB suggests 'night-jar' (so NEB), for which see
NIGHT HAWK.

The screech owl, Strix flammea, lives in Palestine in lonely
places.

The night-hag, Lilith (so JB), was believed to be a female night-
demon, which haunted the people of Edom. Originally Lilith was
the name of a female demon controlling the gale. Known also from
Babylonian legends, she was said to live in the deserts from which
she attacked human beings. Because of the resemblance between
lilith and the Hebrew word for 'night', layil, she was said to be a
night-demon.

REFERENCE: Is 34.14

Night Hawk, Short-eared Owl Caprimulgus europæus, Asio flammeus

Hebrew: taḥmaṣ

DESCRIPTION: The only certain thing to be said about the taḥmaṣ
bird is that it was unclean to the Israelites according to the Law.
Modern scholars disagree upon its identity. KB suggests some
kind of owl; Feliks, in BHH, a falcon; BDB, quoting Bochart, the male
ostrich.

The meaning of the word is uncertain. S. R. Driver derives
the name from a Hb root ḥamaṣ, 'violence', and suggests a predatory bird.

In HDB Driver suggests the short-eared owl (so NEB), though
it is rare and perhaps only a winter visitor to Palestine. JB has
'screech owl'.

RSV translates 'night hawk', which is the goatsucker, Capri-
mulgus europaeus, a migratory bird, dark-coloured and short-
legged, which hunts insects at night. During the day it rests on
branches.

REFERENCES: Lv 11.16; Dt 14.15

Onycha Strombus

Hebrew: sheheleth

DESCRIPTION: LXX renders the Hb word by onyx, which literally
means a nail or anything of the shape of a nail, for instance the shell
of a cockle or mollusc. Cf NEB 'aromatic shell'.

The context in Exodus refers to an ingredient of the incense to
be burnt on the altar. Certain species of molluscs (of the Strombus
family) which live in warm shallow water in the Mediterranean and
Red Seas, when burnt give off an aromatic but pungent smoke.

Others take onycha as a kind of rock rose (Cistus sp.). See
MYRRH.

REFERENCE: Ex 30.34

Ostrich Struthio camelus

Hebrew: ya'en, ya'anah, bath hayya'anah, renanim

DESCRIPTION: The Hb ya'anah is connected by some with an Arabic
word meaning 'desert', by others with an Aramaic word which means
'greed'. Bath hayya'anah is thus 'the daughter of the desert', i. e.
a desert fowl (cf NEB 'desert owl'), or a greedy bird. The identification with 'ostrich' (RV, RSV and JB) goes back to the LXX and the
Targum. Driver in HDB, however, thinks that bath hayya'anah is
most probably the owl (as in AV) and suggests the eagle owl. He rejects the translation 'ostrich' (though accepting it for ya'en and
renanim, as does NEB) on the grounds that the ostrich does not need

[60]

water (Is 43.20, cf 34.13), does not haunt ruins (Is 13.21; Je 50.39) and does not wail as owls do (Mi 1.8).

The Hb word renanim, used only in Job 39.13, may be derived from a root which means 'to give a ringing cry', and may thus be an allusion to the hoarse complaining cry uttered by the bird at night. The 'mourning' mentioned in Mi 1.8, says Bodenheimer, may well be that of an owl.

The passage in Job 39 contains a detailed description of the habits of the ostrich: the eggs are laid in a hollow in the sand, where they are hatched by the heat of the sun and the sand, and at times also by the male bird; the speed with which the ostrich runs, which is helped by the swinging of its wings, sometimes even surpasses that of a mounted hunter. On this see also OTTP, p 90.

REFERENCES: bath hayya'anah: Lv 11.16; Dt 14.15; Job 30.29; Is 13.21; 34.13; 43.20; Je 50.39; Mi 1.8
renanim: Job 39.13
ya'en: La 4.3

Owl

Driver in HDB suggests that there are eight Hb words for owls, arranged in descending order of size in the list of unclean birds in Lv 11.16-18 and Dt 14.15-17, as follows:

1. bath hayya'anah: 'eagle owl' (RSV and JB 'ostrich', NEB 'desert owl')
2. tahmas: 'short-eared owl' (NEB; RSV 'nighthawk', JB 'screech owl')
3. shahaph: 'long-eared owl' (NEB; RSV and JB 'seagull')
4. kos: 'tawny owl' (NEB; RSV 'owl' ['little owl' in Dt 14.16]; JB 'owl', 'horned owl', 'night owl')
5. shalakh: 'fisher owl; (NEB; RSV and JB 'cormorant')
6. yanshuph: 'screech owl' (NEB; RSV 'ibis' ['great owl' in Dt 14.16]; JB 'barn owl')
7. tinshemeth: 'little owl' (NEB; RSV 'water hen', JB 'ibis')
8. qa'ath: 'scops owl' (RSV and JB 'pelican', NEB 'horned owl')

All owls would be unclean as predators feeding on raw flesh.

There are two other words translated 'owl' in English versions. qippoz in Is 34.15 is most likely 'arrowsnake' (so RV; JB 'viper') and not 'owl' (AV and RSV). See ARROWSNAKE, but see also PARTRIDGE (so NEB). lilith in Is 34.14 is the nightjar (NEB and RSV 'night hag') and not the screech owl (AV). JB transliterates.

The identification of the different species of owls is very difficult. The fact that owls chiefly dwell in ruins and deserted places, and that the hoot of an owl caused much superstitious fear, has made it a symbol of desolation and devastation in the Bible.

Ox, Cow bos

Hebrew: baqar (ox, cattle, herd), shor (single head of cattle), par (young bull), parah (cow), 'eghel (calf), 'eghlah (heifer), ?eleph (cattle), ?abbir (lit: strong, mighty)

Greek: bous, tauros, ktēnos, damalis (heifer), moschos (calf), thremma (cattle), sitista (cattle that have been fattened)

DESCRIPTION: An interesting point about the description of this animal in the OT is the emphasis on its beauty. This has made some commentators think of old Egyptian and Assyrian illustrations, showing a stately animal not unlike the Indian zebu, or small humped ox.

Egypt was rich in cattle, especially in the Delta area, Goshen, where the Hebrews settled under Joseph. Abraham received oxen as a gift from Pharoah when he went into Egypt (Gn 12.14-16). In Palestine cattle grazed on the plains (e. g. the plain of Sharon), in Bashan and in Gilead. The behaviour and habits of cattle are described in the book of the herdsman Amos.

The habit of fattening cattle for special purposes is mentioned in 1 K 1.9; 4.23; Mt 22.4; Lk 15.23; cf 1 S 28.24 ('eghel marbeq, 'a stall-fattened calf'). marbeq literally means 'a tying place'. The cattle that were to be fattened were not intended to get too much exercise.

[62]

Cattle were used not only for sacrificial purposes and for food, but also as draught animals (e. g. Lk 14.19) and for treading out grain (Dt 25.4; 1 Co 9.9; 1 Ti 5.18).

The milk of the cow is often mentioned as food (Gn 18.8; Jg 4.19). Even cheese is mentioned (Job 10.10); Duhm comments, 'a sample of ancient physiology', the formation of the embryo in the womb explained in terms of the curdling of cheese.

ʔabbir in Jg 5.22 is 'bull' or 'horse'; in Is 10.13 keʔabbir is translated by some 'like a mighty man', more correctly RSV and NEB 'like a bull'.

In Jn 4.12 AG explain thremma as 'domesticated animal, especially sheep or goat'.

REFERENCES: ʔeleph: Dt 7.13; 28.4,18,51; Ps 8.7; 50.10; Pr 14.4;
      Is 30.24
ʔabbir signifying 'bull': Ps 22.12; 50.13; Is 10.13;
      34.7; Je 46.15
For other Hb words consult a concordance
teʔo: see IBEX
bous: Lk 13.15; 14.5,19; Jn 2.14,15; 1 Co 9.9; 1 Ti 5.18
tauros: Mt 22.4; Ac 14.13; He 9.13; 10.4
ktēnos: cattle: Rv 18.13; animals used for riding:
      Lk 10.34; Ac 23.24; domesticated animals:
      1 Co 15.39
moschos: Lk 15.23,27,30; He 9.12,19; Rv 4.7
moschopoieō: 'to make a calf' Ac 7.41
sitista: Mt 22.4. damalis: He 9.13
thremma: Jn 4.12

DIFFICULT PASSAGES: reʔem: Nu 23.22; 24.8; Dt 33.17; Job 39.9; Ps 22.21; 29.6; 92.10; Is 34.7 is generally translated 'wild ox' (AV 'unicorn'), Bos primigenius, which in ancient times was hunted by Assyrian kings. The Akkadian word rīmu undoubtedly stands for the aurochs, or wild ox. Some commentators have connected the Hb word with the Arabic rim 'antelope'. This animal, however, is rather shy and easy to tame, which does not fit the OT description of a wild, strong and untamable animal.

Partridge   Caccabis chukar or Ammoperdix heyi

Hebrew: qore?

DESCRIPTION: The rock partridge or Caccabis chukar was a favourite game bird in Biblical times. It was hunted in the mountains of Palestine, as its delicate flesh makes excellent eating. Another species which is the only partridge found in the desert of Engedi (cf 1 S 26.20) is the sand partridge, Ammoperdix heyi. The wilderness of Ziph (1 S 26.2) is around Engedi.

The rock partridge is a colourful bird with red legs and bill, and a white throat edged with a black line.

The sand partridge is of medium size, with yellow feet. The male has sandy buff plumage, the upper tail coverts pencilled and barred with brown, the under-surface chestnut and white; the female is greyish buff. This partridge is a great runner and speeds along the ground when it is chased, until it becomes exhausted and can be knocked down by the hunter's stick.

The Hb name of the partridge, qore?, literally means 'the caller', alluding to the peculiar call the bird makes when frightened.

The partridge is often snared by means of a decoy. Ecclesiasticus 11.30 mentions a 'decoy partridge in a cage' which indicates the custom of concealing a cage somewhere in the hunting area, with a captured bird inside which with its call notes will attract wild birds.

Je 17.11, 'the partridge that gathers a brood which she did not hatch', refers to an ancient belief that the partridge steals eggs from other nests but that hatched fledglings return to their own mother. This erroneous idea may be due to the fact that the hen lays an unusually large number of eggs (a nest containing 26 has been found); or to the fact that the chukar or rock partridge lays two clutches, one for the cock to incubate. Jeremiah and 1 Samuel are therefore (not surprisingly) using the same Hb word to describe two different species.

Driver in HDB suggests that qippoz (see ARROWSNAKE) may be a variety of the sand partridge Caccabis sinaica, which hops or leaps away with great agility when disturbed.

REFERENCES: 1 S 26.20; Je 17.11

DIFFICULT PASSAGE: Jg 15.19 'en haqqore? should not be translated 'partridge well', but 'the caller's well', as indicated in the RSV note, as it commemorates Samson's calling on God for help.

Pelican Pelicanus onocrotalus

Hebrew: qa?ath

DESCRIPTION: The Hb qa?ath is one of the numerous unclean birds in Lv 11 and Dt 14 whose identification is doubtful. Many scholars nowadays translate 'pelican', most of them however noting that the meaning of the word is uncertain. One reason for this is that the pelican frequents rivers and lakes rather than ruins, as it is said to in Is 34 and Zeph 2.

The only sure thing we can say about the Hb word is that it stands for an unclean bird, which dwells in ruins, and that the word may be derived from a root 'to throw out', consequently 'a vomiter', which is taken by commentators to allude to the pelican's alleged habit of throwing up food for its young from its crop.

The pelican is a picturesque bird with snowy white feathers, broad wings the expansion of which is 3.6 to 3.9 m, and a large yellow bill. 'When it sits motionless at the edge of a swamp, its head against its breast, digesting the fishes it has scooped up in its pouch, it becomes the very image of brooding sorrow' (Parmelee, p 169).

Driver in HDB suggests the scops owl, otus scops, which is common in olive groves and about ruins in Palestine. qa?ath may then be an onomatopoeic word to represent hooting. NEB has 'horned owl' ('desert owl' in Ps 102.6); RSV 'pelican' in Leviticus and Deuteronomy, elsewhere 'vulture' or 'hawk'.

REFERENCES: Lv 11.18; Dt 14.17; Ps 102.6; Is 34.11; Zeph 2.14

Porcupine, Bittern   Hystrix cristata (European porcupine)

Botaurus stellaris (bittern)

Hebrew: qippodh

DESCRIPTION: The Hb qippodh may be derived from a verb which means 'to roll up'; this has led to the traditional identification with the porcupine. Three species are found in Palestine, among them Hystrix cristata.

The context of the references indicates that we have to do with an animal which haunts desolate places. This, in addition to the allusion to 'pools of water' in Is 14.23, has led some translators to render the word 'bittern', a bird with long neck and legs, which lives near ponds and moors; its weird and mournful cries have always caused superstitious dread. No definite decision as to identification can be made.

Driver in HDB rejects 'porcupine' on the grounds that it could scarcely 'lodge in the capitals' of pillars in Nineveh (Zeph 2.14). 'Bittern' might fit the 'pools of water' in Is 14.23 but not the desolate places of the other two passages. He suggests that the meaning 'rolled up' of qippodh would suit the bustard (otis), which has a bunched-up neck that swells in some species into a ruff in the breeding season. At least three species are seen in Palestine, shy birds which are usually found in waste ground, open places or the desert edge. NEB translates 'bustard'.

AV has 'bittern'. RV, following LXX and Vulgate, has 'porcupine'. RSV has 'porcupine' in Is 34.11 and 'hedgehog' elsewhere. JB has 'hedgehog' in Isaiah, 'heron' in Zephaniah.

REFERENCES: Is 14.23; 34.11; Zeph 2.14

Quail Coturnix coturnix

Hebrew: selaw

DESCRIPTION: All commentators are now in agreement with regard to the identification of this bird. The quail is a small migratory

bird, 19 cm long.   It is brown or sandy in colour with yellowish
streaks, and comes to Palestine during March and April in enormous
flocks.   In its flight it usually follows the wind, but if the wind suddenly changes, the entire flock may be driven to the ground where
it lies exhausted and can easily be caught or killed.

The 'spreading out' mentioned in Nu 11 was for the purpose of
drying the flesh and thus preserving it for future use.

Bodenheimer (in ID) points out that the reference in Nu 11.33 to
a plague caused by the eating of quails has medico-historical support.

REFERENCES: Ex 16.13; Nu 11.31, 32; Ps 105.40

Quail (*Coturnix coturnix*)

Raven Corvidæ

Hebrew: 'orebh   Greek: korax

DESCRIPTION: As a wise sailor Noah made his reckoning by the
flight of the birds, sending out a raven and not a dove as his first
messenger, because the raven is a highly developed bird and much

hardier than the dove. The raven did not return to the ark. It was able to survive without human help as it feeds on carrion and would 'find enough to eat in the floating wreckage of a flooded world' (Parmelee, p 55).

The raven is listed among the unclean birds. Its nest is usually found in solitary places. It is a common bird all over Palestine, has a beautiful black colour and is about 62 cm long. According to Lv 11, the Hb word is a general name for all ravens (Corvidæ).

REFERENCES: <u>'orebh</u>: Gn 8.7; Lv 11.15; Dt 14.14; 1 K 17.4, 6; Job 38. 41; Ps 147.9; Pr 30.17; SS 5.11; Is 34.11. (Jg 7.25 and Is 10.26 refer to place names.) <u>korax</u>: Lk 12.24

DIFFICULT PASSAGE: The miracle by the brook Cherith (1 K 17),

Raven (*Corvidæ*)

where the ravens brought Elijah bread and meat every morning and evening, has been interpreted in a naturalistic way by some commentators: they read 'Arabs' instead of 'ravens'. This is possible by changing the vowels, as the consonants of the words 'Arabs' and 'ravens' are the same in Hebrew.

Rock badger (*Procavia syriacus*)

Rock Badger, Syrian Coney   Procavia syriacus

Hebrew: shaphan

DESCRIPTION: Modern translators generally agree in identifying this animal with the rock badger, although it does not belong to the ruminants among which it is mentioned in Lv 11. When chewing it moves its jaws in a way that resembles a ruminant.

The rock badger lives among rocks from the Dead Sea valley to Mt. Hermon. Older European translators, such as Luther and AV, who were not familiar with this animal, thought it to be the rabbit. The rock badger is a herbivorous animal about the size of a hare. It belongs to the order of Hyracoidea and to the group of the subungulates. It has no hoofs but broad nails. The toes, four on the fore-legs and three on the back limbs, are connected with skin almost like a web. Under its feet it has pads like sucking-discs which enable it to keep its footing on slippery rocks. Its habits are gregarious, rather like those of the marmot. Its fur is yellow and brown, and it has short ears and a very small tail.

JB translates 'hyrax' ('rock rabbit' in Proverbs).

REFERENCES: Lv 11.5; Dt 14.7; Ps 104.18; Pr 30.26

Scorpion   Buthus quinquestriatus

Hebrew: 'aqrabh   Greek: skorpios

DESCRIPTION: The scorpion belongs to the order of Arachnida and is akin to the spider. It is quite common in Mediterranean countries and was also in Palestine in Biblical times, as is shown by an ascent south of the Dead Sea named Akrabbim (Nu 34.4; Jos 15.3; Jg 1.36).

It is a small animal with eight legs like a spider. Its main characteristics are its two claws, like a lobster's, with which it catches and holds its prey, and its long jointed tail which can be curled up over its head and which contains the venom gland. The tail also has a sting, which is extremely painful, and can on occasion even be dangerous to man (Rv 9.5, 10). It feeds on locusts and beetles.

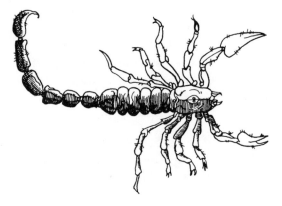

Scorpion (*Buthus*)

Hauck points out that when contracted at rest a scorpion may have some similarity to an egg, so that a person reaching for an egg in the dark in a small house might make a serious mistake.

Many species of scorpion are found in Palestine, from 4 to 20 cm long.

REFERENCES: 'aqrabh: Nu 34.4; Dt 8.15; Jos 15.3; Jg 1.36;
               1 K 12.11,14; 2 Ch 10.11,14; Ezk 2.6
            skorpios: Lk 10.19; 11.12; Rv 9.3,5,10

DIFFICULT PASSAGES: ma'aleh 'aqrabbim (Nu 34.4; Jos 15.3; Jg 1.36) is a geographical name which indicates the presence of the animal, as stated above. The word 'aqrabh in 1 Kings and 2 Chronicles refers not to the animal but to a whip called a 'scorpion'.

Sea Gull, Tern   Larus or Sterna fluviatilis

Hebrew: shaḥaph

DESCRIPTION: The root of the Hb word shaḥaph suggests the meaning 'thin' or 'lean', and this, of course, is a good description of the common tern, Sterna fluviatilis.

Today it is the Hb name for 'gull', but, as Bodenheimer says, whether it was so in Biblical times is not certain.

Vulgate, LXX, RSV and JB translate 'seagull', AV has 'cuckoo', and Driver (followed by NEB) suggests 'long-eared owl', Asio otus.

REFERENCES: Lv 11.16; Dt 14.15

Serpent, Viper, Adder, Leviathan

Bitis varietans (Cerastes cornuta) (Naja haje) (Echis colorata)

Hebrew: naḥash, ?eph'eh, tsepha', pethen, shephiphon, tannin, sharaph, liwyathan, 'akhshubh, zoḥeleth

Greek: ophis, echidna, herpeton, aspis

DESCRIPTION: Serpents are among the most widespread reptiles and are to be found in all continents; they decrease in number and species towards the poles, but increase as one approaches the equator.

Thirty-three different species have been found in Palestine and neighbouring countries, twenty of which are poisonous. 'The poison of vipers' (Ps 140.3) makes them feared by the inhabitants. The poison of e.g. the cobra (Naja haje) is dangerous and may lead to death within half an hour. The serpent's weapon of attack is its poison fang, but in Biblical times it was believed to be the tongue (Job 20.16; Ps 140.3). Other dangerous characteristics of the serpent noticed by Biblical writers are its inconspicuous way of moving and the ease with which it hides itself. So it becomes a symbol of the unexpectedness of the Day of the Lord (Am 5.19) and an illustration of the treachery and subtlety of both man and the devil (Mt 3.7; Gn 3.1).

tsepha': BDB says that the identification of this word is difficult. He refers to Tristram, who suggests daboia xanthina, a venomous viper, but adds that vipers do not lay eggs, and quotes Furrer who proposes ailurophis vivax. AV has 'cockatrice'; RSV 'viper'; JB 'adder', 'basilisk' and 'viper'; NEB usually 'viper'.

pethen is usually rendered 'asp' or 'cobra' (Naja haje).

?eph'eh, according to Bodenheimer, is identified in modern Hb with the carpet viper, Echis colorata, and this may also be the Biblical meaning. The carpet viper is a poisonous snake, quite common in the Jericho plain. RSV, JB and NEB all have 'viper' (NEB 'sand-viper' in Is 30).

REFERENCES: naḥash: Consult a concordance
ʔeph'eh: Job 20.16; Is 30.6; 59.5
tsepha': Pr 23.32; Is 11.8; 14.29; 59.5; Je 8.17
pethen: Dt 32.33; Job 20.14,16; Ps 58.4; 91.13; Is 11.8
shephiphon: Gn 49.17
tannin: Gn 1.21; Ne 2.13; Job 7.12; Ps 74.13; 148.7;
Is 27.1; 51.9; Je 51.34; La 4.3; Ezk 29.3; 32.2 (in all
these passages the Hb word stands for some 'sea
monster'; only in the following passages should
tannin be translated 'serpent': Ex 7.9,10,12; Dt
32.33; Ps 91.13)
sharaph: Nu 21.6, 8; Dt 8.15; Is 14.29 (In Is 6.2,6 it
should be translated 'seraphim'.)
liwyathan: Job 3.8; 41.1; Ps 74.14; 104.26; Is 27.1
ophis: Mt 7.10; 10.16; 23.33; Mk 16.18; Lk 10.19; 11.11;
Jn 3.14; 1 Co 10.9; 2 Co 11.3; Rv 9.19; 12.9,14f; 20.2
echidna: Mt 3.7; 12.34; 23.33; Lk 3.7; Ac 28.3
herpeton: Ac 10.12; 11.16; Ro 1.23; Jas 3.7
aspis: Ro 3.13

DIFFICULT PASSAGES: 1 K 1.9: ʔeben zoḥeleth is the name of a
place in the neighbourhood of Jerusalem. RSV and JB render 'The
Serpent's Stone', because the word may be derived from zaḥal, 'to
creep, to crawl' (cf Dt 32.24; Mi 7.17). NEB transliterates 'the stone
Zoheleth'.

Ps 140.3: 'akhshubh is 'viper' or 'spider'. See SPIDER.

liwyathan, Leviathan, is derived from a word which means 'to
wind'. Is 27.1 and Ps 74.14 are connected with the mythological background of the Israelites, of which we know very little. Bodenheimer
says it is the primordial dragon known in Canaanite mythology. It
may be influenced by the Babylonian creation myth, that the creation
of the world was caused by God's victory over a snake or a dragon
with seven heads. In this way order was introduced. The Talmud,
commenting on these two passages, talks of a male and a female
leviathan as a huge fish or sea monster. The female leviathan has
been killed, the male will be killed by the angel Michael on the day
of judgment.

[73]

The derivation of the word suggests a snake or fish. Job 3.8 mentions leviathan in a way that suggests to some commentators the Egyptian army, but it may also be that the poet has in mind a heavenly snake-monster, which by magic can be brought to darken the heaven.

Job 41.1 is often explained as the crocodile (cf JB note), but the derivation of the word does not fit the crocodile, whose neck and spine are entirely stiff, so that a man on land can escape from it easily by running a zigzag course. Some commentators have pointed out that 'drawing out the tongue with a cord' would not apply in ancient times, because the crocodile was thought to have no tongue. It does have one, but it is flat and fastened to the lower jaw.

It was once thought that the tongue of the snake was poisonous and that the poisonous snake bit with its tongue. This might have led to the translation 'snake'.

Some of the words in Job 41: 'merchants', 'harpoons', 'fishing spears' in vv 6ff suggest fishing, and some translate liwyathan by 'whale' (so NEB). Whales have often been caught in the Mediterranean, both in ancient and recent times. A whale is too heavy to be caught by a hook (v 1), and its hide cannot be penetrated by barbs. Even the difficult v 5 can be made to suit the context, because it is said that when fishermen in the Nile have caught a rare fish and wish to show it, they keep it alive by leaving it in the water after fastening a ring to its nose and tying it up with a line. This can scarcely be done to a whale. Ps 104.26 can, of course, be translated 'whale'.

It should be borne in mind that all quotations dealing with leviathan are poetical.

tannin, 'sea monster' or 'serpent' should be carefully distinguished from tannim, 'jackal' or possibly 'wolf'. It is often confused in the Masoretic text. In La 4.3 the kethib tannin (AV) is more likely than the qere tannim (RSV).

echidna in Ac 28.3 is probably a non-poisonous snake with small teeth.

[74]

Sheep (*Ovis laticaudata*)

Sheep, Lamb, Ram   Ovis laticaudata

Hebrew: seh plural, tso?n (small cattle, sheep or goats), zemer
(mountain sheep), raḥel (ewe), kebhes (lamb), ?ayil (ram),
ṭaleh (lamb), kar (lamb, ram), yobhel (ram, ram's horn,
cornet)

Aramaic: dekhar (ram), ?immar (lamb)

Greek: amnos (lamb), probaton (small cattle, sheep), probation
(little sheep), arēn (lamb), arnion (lamb), pascha (the
Paschal lamb)

DESCRIPTION: The sheep mentioned in the Bible is usually the
broad-tailed sheep (Ovis laticaudata). Whereas the tail of other
sheep is short, that of the broad-tailed is long and broad, containing
a mass of fat which may weigh up to 13 kg. The fat tail was used as
a sacrifice, Ex 29.22; Lv 3.9; 7.3; 8.25; 9.19. Only the ram of this
species has horns, but there are other varieties of sheep in Palestine,
of which the ewe also has horns. The ram's horns might be used as
trumpets (Jos 6.4) or as oil-containers (1 S 16.1).

In the Bible sheep are often mentioned as 'small cattle', which
includes goats as well. Of these the sheep were more numerous and
important. The rich man Nabal had 3,000 sheep and 1,000 goats

(1 S 25.2).   The man of whom Jesus spoke in the parable (Lk 15.4) who
had only 100 sheep, could not afford to lose a single one of them.

Most sheep were white (Ps 147.16; Is 1.18; Dn 7.9; Rv 1.14)

REFERENCES: For seh and tso?n consult a concordance
                     zemer: Dt 14.5
                     raḥel: Gn 31.38; 32.14; SS 6.6; Is 53.7
                     For kebhes, ?ayil and yobhel consult a concordance
                     ṭaleh: 1 S 7.9; Is 40.11; 65.25
                     kar: Dt 32.14; 1 S 15.9; 2 K 3.4; Is 16.1; 34.6; Je 51.40;
                        Ezk 27.21; 39.18; Am 6.4
                     dekhar: Ezra 6.9,17; 7.17
                     ?immar: Ezra 6.9,17; 7.17
                     amnos: Jn 1.29, 36; Ac 8.32; 1 P 1.19
                     For probaton consult a concordance
                     pascha: Mk 14.12; Lk 22.7; 1 Co 5.7
                     probation: Jn 21.16,17
                     arēn: Lk 10.3
                     arnion: Jn 21.15, and 29 times in Revelation

DIFFICULT PASSAGES: Dt 14.5: RSV and JB, following Tristram,
translate zemer as 'mountain sheep' (Ovis tragelaphus).   NEB has
'rock-goat'. The 'chamois' of AV and RV does not occur in the area.

For 1 S 9.24, see OTTP, p 28.

Snail Mollusca

Hebrew: shabbelul

DESCRIPTION: According to a tradition dating from early times,
this word has been identified with the snail. Scholars have derived
the name from the verb balal, 'to waste away, to fade away'.
Wellhausen renders the sentence: 'Like the snail that dissolves as
it crawls'. JB has 'slug'. In modern Hb the word stands for 'snail',
but the possibility remains that in the Bible, where it occurs only
once, it may have no relation to any animal. Driver (Journal of

[76]

Theological Studies, XXXIV, 41f) argues for the meaning 'miscarriage', cf 'untimely birth' in the parallel line. NEB 'abortive birth'.

REFERENCE: Ps 58.8

Snail (*Mollusca*)

Sparrow Passer domesticus

Hebrew: tsippor (?)   Greek: strouthion

DESCRIPTION: The sparrow, which always builds its nest close to the home of man, is so common all over the world that a description of it is unnecessary.

According to the Law of Moses the Jews were not forbidden to eat the flesh of the sparrow, and the words of Jesus: 'Are not two sparrows sold for a penny?' indicate that this was a cheap and common food for the ordinary man in Palestine. Jesus directs his words not to the powerful and rich, but to the worried and care-worn. This is why he makes use of the sparrow, a cheap and common creature, as an illustration.

Some translators also render the Hb word tsippor as 'sparrow'. This word is derived from a root meaning 'to cheep or whistle', so that tsippor probably stands for 'bird' in general, leaving it to the context to decide, if possible, what kind of bird is referred to.

The sparrow's habit of staying close to human living quarters has caused many commentators to translate tsippor 'sparrow' in Ps 84.3 and Ec 12.4 (so RSV, JB in Ps, and NEB).

REFERENCES: For tsippor consult a concordance
            strouthion: Mt 10.29, 31; Lk 12.6, 7

Spider   Aranea

Hebrew: 'akkabhish

DESCRIPTION: There are 600 to 700 species of Arachnida in present-day Palestine. Peculiar to the spider is the web, referred to in the passages mentioned below.

REFERENCES: Job 8.14; Is 59.5

DIFFICULT PASSAGES: Ps 140.3: The Hb word 'akhshubh is usually translated 'asp', 'viper'. But some modern scholars (e. g. Bodenheimer) maintain that this is the same word as 'akkabhish (so NEB, 'spiders' poison'). Some linguists say that it is a corrupted form of 'akkabhish.

Pr 30.28: The Hb semamith is often translated 'lizard' (so RV, RSV, JB and NEB), but Bodenheimer and others understand it from the context to be the spider. Whether the text supports Bodenheimer's contention is a matter for conjecture.

Spider (*Aranea*)

Stork   Ciconia alba, Ciconia nigra

Hebrew: ḥaṣidhah

DESCRIPTION: The Hb name may be derived from a root which means 'goodness, kindness', and the bird was probably so called because it was considered to be affectionate to its young, in contrast to the ostrich (q. v.).

The stork is a migratory bird (Je 8.7), spending its winters in south-east Africa, and it is known all over Europe and Asia, where it feeds on smaller reptiles and fish in swamps and creeks. However, it is generally omnivorous, so that it was considered unclean by the Law of Moses. It is a big bird, 1.2 m high, with a long red bill and legs, a long neck and large black wings (Zech 5.9). The black stork is entirely black, except for the bill and legs. In the Orient the stork often builds on high trees (Ps 104.17).

REFERENCES: Lv 11.19; Dt 14.18; Job 39.13; Ps 104.17; Je 8.7; Zech 5.9

DIFFICULT PASSAGE: For Job 39.13 see OTTP, p 90. RSV here translates ḥeṣidhah 'of love', RV 'kindly'. Hoffman's emendation ḥaṣerah ('are pinions and plumage lacking?') makes good sense.

Stork (*Ciconia alba*)

Swallow and Swift Hirundo rustica, Cypselus apus

Hebrew: deror, ṣuṣ, ṣiṣ

DESCRIPTION: Previous Bible translators did not distinguish between deror and ṣuṣ or ṣiṣ, but Tristram has underlined two peculiarities about the swallow and the swift, as he met them in Palestine, which may be of importance when it comes to an identification of the bird in question.

One is that the swallows of Palestine are to a large extent resident, and this circumstance makes it less likely that the swallow is referred to in Je 8.7, where the ṣuṣ is said to 'keep the time of its coming'. The swift, on the other hand, is a migratory bird. Secondly, the twittering of a swallow is not a particularly striking illustration of King Hezekiah's cry of pain (Is 38.14), whereas the swift of Palestine is said to have a note very much like a piercing human scream (see Parmelee, p 174).

It therefore seems advisable to translate the words ṣuṣ and ṣiṣ 'swift', in spite of RV, RSV and JB 'swallow'. NEB has 'swift' for ṣiṣ but 'dove' for ṣuṣ. These words are used in modern Hb for 'swift'. deror was used in the medieval Hb commentaries for 'swallow'; it now means 'sparrow'. It seems practical to translate 'swallow', as do RSV, JB, NEB.

REFERENCES: deror: Ps 84.3; Pr 26.2
ṣuṣ: Is 38.14
ṣiṣ: Jer 8.7

Swine, Pig Sus scrofa

Hebrew: ḥazir   Greek: choiros, hus

DESCRIPTION: Since the swine was an unclean animal and Jews were forbidden to eat its flesh (Lv 11.7; Dt 14.8), the swine mentioned in the Bible must in most cases have been the wild pig, which is still common in Palestine (Martin Noth). With regard to Mk 5 and parallels, see below. The pig is omnivorous, even eating carrion, and this may be enough to explain the law. However, it is remarkable that its unsavoury aspect is emphasized in the comparatively few passages where it is mentioned. The pig became the symbol of filthiness and paganism (Pr 11.22; Mt 7.6; 2 P 2.22). During the Babylonian captivity the people were led astray and ate pork (Is 65. 2-4). The fact that the Prodigal Son was sent into 'the fields to feed swine' indicates how deeply he was humilated (Lk 15.15).

REFERENCES: ḥazir: Lv 11.7; Dt 14.8; Ps 80.13; Pr 11.22; Is 65.4;
           66.3,17
      choiros: Mt 7.6; 8.30-32; Mk 5.11-13,16; Lk 8.32f;
           15.15f
      hus: 2 P 2.22

DIFFICULT PASSAGES: Is 66.3: Some commentators add before dam-ḥazir the word nosek referring to the libation of pig's blood. Paul Volz, who thinks that the addition makes the verse too long, reads ḥomed instead of dam, which gives the translation 'covetous of pork'.

    Mk 5.13 and parallels: see 'A Translator's Handbook on Mark', p 163. Herdsmen and herds of pigs were not supposed to be found in Jewish territory, but only among Gentile neighbours.

Swine (*Sus scrofa*)

Vulture (Eagle) Gyps fulvus, Gypaetus barbatus

Hebrew: nesher (Aramaic: neshar), da?ah, pereṣ, raham,
'ozniyah

Greek: aetos

DESCRIPTION: The vulture is a large bird of prey with a wing-
spread of as much as 2 m. At one time it could be seen everywhere
in Palestine soaring at an immense height (Tristram). Head and
neck are featherless, and it feeds mostly on carrion.

Zoologists of ancient times did not distinguish between the different large birds of prey. Aristotle (4th cent BC) and Pliny (1st
cent AD) class the vulture among the eagles. The context and the
description of the bird must therefore decide which translation

Vulture (*Aquila chrysætus*)

should be chosen. In modern times eight species of eagle and four species of vulture are found in Palestine.

In the list of clean and unclean birds, it is reasonable to translate nesher 'eagle' and pereş 'vulture' (Lv 11.13; Dt 14.12).

The imperial eagle, Aquila heliaca, common in Palestine, is almost certainly the bird described in Pr 23.5 as flying towards heaven. 2 S 1.23; Je 4.13 and La 4.19 (NEB 'vulture') may refer to this species, or to the golden eagle, Aquila chrysaetus, the female of which has been known to catch her young on her wings, as described in Ex 19.4; Dt 32.11.

Lv 11.14: da?ah is translated gups 'vulture' in the LXX and milvus 'kite' in the Vulgate, which is probably the correct translation; so RSV, JB and NEB.

Lv 11.18 and Dt 14.12: raham 'carrion vulture' (vultur percnopterus) as in RSV may well be correct (so Bertholet). Driver in HDB, however, thinks 'vulture' unlikely because of its size and the position of raham in the list of birds in Lv 11.18. The root r-h-m describes a black and white object, and may therefore refer to the osprey, Pandion haliaetus, which fits the 'black and white' description. Its habits also would suggest its place in the list between predatory owls on the one hand and fisher birds like stork and heron on the other.

In Lv 11.13 and Dt 14.12 'ozniyah is also listed as a bird of prey. It is difficult to identify. Tristram suggests the osprey; others think it is the bearded vulture, Gypaetus barbatus; Driver in HDB suggests the short-toed eagle.

In passages in which the word nesher occurs, unless specific characteristics of the vulture are described, the word should be translated 'eagle'. Such characteristics are:

1) feeding on carrion. Cf Pr 30.17, where perhaps there is also an allusion to the vulture's habit of starting on the eyes or other soft parts of the victim's body. Ho 8.1 may describe a vulture soaring over a battlefield filled with corpses, but many commentators emend the text and instead of 'eagle' or 'vulture' read 'watchman' (notser); so JB.

2) baldness of head and neck. Mi 1.16 ought therefore to be translated 'vulture' (i. e. the griffon-vulture, gyps fulvus, of Ezk 17.3, 7, because the griffon-vulture is remarkable for its large wing-spread) as in JB and NEB, and not as in RSV 'eagle'.

3) nesting on cliffs. Job 39.27f; Je 49.16

4) gathering from a distance at the prospect of carrion. Dt 28.49; Je 49.22; Hbk 1.8

Most passages in which the word nesher occurs speak of the beauty and majesty of a bird of prey, which can most adequately be attributed to the eagle. This is also true of the two passages from the book of Daniel (neshar).

aetos in Mt 24.28 and Lk 17.37 should be rendered 'vulture' and in Revelation probably 'eagle'.

Driver's more or less tentative identifications in HDB may be summarized as follows:

nesher - imperial eagle, Aquila heliaca, or golden eagle, Aquila chrysaetus, or griffon-vulture, Gyps fulvus, according to context.
da?ah - kite, Milvus migrans.
peres - vulture, perhaps Arrian's vulture, Gypaëtus barbatus. RSV 'ossifrage', JB 'griffon', NEB 'black vulture'.
raham - ossifrage or osprey, Pandion haliaetus, so NEB. RSV 'vulture', JB 'white vulture'.
'ozniyah - short-toed eagle, Circaetus gallicus. RSV and JB 'osprey', NEB 'bearded vulture'.

REFERENCES: nesher: Ex 19.4; Lv 11.13; Dt 14.12; 28.49; 32.11; 2 S 1.23; Job 9.26; 39.27; Ps 103.5; Pr 23.5; 30.17, 19; Is 40.31; Je 4.13; 48.40; 49.16, 22; La 4.19; Ezk 1.10; 10.14; 17.3, 7; Ho 8.1; Ob 4; Mi 1.16; Hbk 1.8
neshar: Dn 4.33; 7.4
da?ah: Lv 11.14
peres: Lv 11.13; Dt 14.12
raham: Lv 11.18; Dt 14.17

'ozniyah: Lv 11.13; Dt 14.12
aetos: Mt 24.28; Lk 17.37; Rv 4.7; 8.13; 12.14

Wolf (*Canis lupus*)

Wolf Canis lupus

Hebrew: ze?ebh   Greek: lukos

DESCRIPTION: The wolf was common in Palestine in Biblical times. It is a restless animal, hunting its prey mainly by night. In northern winters wolves hunt in packs, but in summer and in warm countries the wolf is a solitary hunter. Biblical accounts of Palestinian shepherds tell of many bloody fights between man and wolf.

The wolf's habit of seeking its prey at night is mentioned in Je 5.6; Hbk 1.8 and Zeph 3.3: 'evening wolves'. The latter passage also alludes to the proverbial greediness of the wolf. Both its courage and also its cruelty are in the mind of the patriarch Jacob when he predicts the fate of the tribe of Benjamin, Gn 49.27.

The strategy of the wolf is described in Jn 10.12: 'stealing' or 'snatching' and 'scattering' the flock.

The word is used in the Bible not only in a literal sense, but often symbolically about men whose qualities in some respects resemble those of the wolf, such as leaders who rob the people, Ezk 22.27, or teachers who deceive their disciples, Mt 7.15; Ac 20.29.

REFERENCES: ze?ebh: Gn 49.27; Jg 7.25; 8.3; Ps 83.11; Is 11.6; 65.25; Je 5.6; Ezk 22.27; Hbk 1.8; Zeph 3.3
lukos: Mt 7.15; 10.16; Lk 10.3; Jn 10.12; Ac 20. 29

DIFFICULT PASSAGES: It should be noted that ze?ebh is used as a proper name in Jg 7.25; 8.3; Ps 83.11.

Worm, Maggot vermis

Hebrew: tole'ah, rimmah   Greek: skōlēx

DESCRIPTION: It is not possible to give a general description, as the context must decide what kind of creature is meant. tole'ah usually stands for a worm that destroys grapes and plants, devours corpses and symbolizes the weakness and insignificance of man.

rimmah is derived from a root meaning 'to grow rotten' and may be understood as a worm which causes or indicates corruption, a maggot. The word symbolizes decay or (Job 25.6) an insignificant man.

REFERENCES: tole'ah: Ex 16.20; Dt 28.39; Job 25.6; Ps 22.6;
Is 14.11; 41.14; 66.24; Jon 4.7 (also found in many passages in Ex, Lv and Nu, for the coccus ilicis or cochineal, an insect producing scarlet dye)
rimmah: Ex 16.24; Job 7.5; 17.14; 21.26; 24.20; 25.6; Is 14.11
skōlēx: Mk 9.48 (perhaps also vv 44 and 46)
skōlēkobrōtos: 'eaten by worms', Ac 12.23

DIFFICULT PASSAGE: For Job 24.20, which literally translated gives no meaning, see OTTP, p 79. It is advisable to read shemo ('his name') instead of rimmah; so RSV and JB.

[86]

Flora of the Bible

Acacia   Acacia raddiana

Hebrew: shiṭṭah

DESCRIPTION: The AV does not identify this tree, but simply transliterates 'shittah' or 'shittim'. Today it is generally recognized that shiṭṭah is identical with the acacia (as rendered by RV, RSV, JB and NEB).

The acacia is a member of the Mimosa family. Four different species are found in Palestine, the most common being the A. rad-

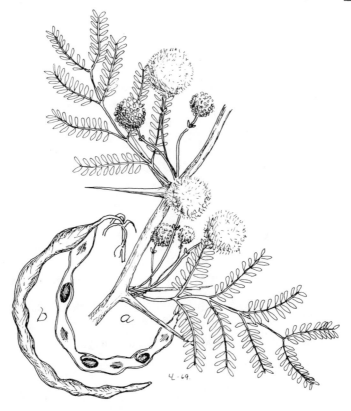

Acacia (*Acacia raddiana*)
a. flowering twig
b. opening pod with seeds

diana, which grows in the valleys around the Dead Sea. It is an evergreen tree, 3 to 5.5 m high, with spiny branches carrying yellow flowers; its wood is very useful for building purposes. The other three species are A. spinocarpa, A. arabica and A. albida.

The word shiṭṭim, plural of shiṭṭah, is sometimes used to designate different localities, as for instance the region east of the river Jordan opposite Jericho: Nu 33.49; Joel 3.18 (a valley).

REFERENCES: Ex 25.5, 10, 13, 23, 28; 26.15, 26, 32, 37; 27.1, 6; 30.1, 5; 35.7, 24; 36.20, 31, 36; 37.1, 4, 10, 15, 25, 28; 38.1, 6; Dt 10.3; Is 41.19

Algum, Almug timber   Juniperus phoenicea excelsa

Hebrew: ʔalgummim,   ʔalmuggim

DESCRIPTION: Traditionally, algum or almug (JB 'algummim', 'almuggim') has been regarded as sandalwood, Pterocarpus santalinus, which may have been imported by King Solomon from southern India and used for the pillars and balustrades of the temple and royal palace. It is a large tree with very hard red wood, which takes a fine polish.

But Josephus says (Antiq. VIII, 7, 1) that the wood used for Solomon's temple and palace was even 'whiter and more shining' than that of the fig tree, so some commentators identify it with Santalum album. However, the white sandal tree, a native of India, is little more than a bush and has no value as timber.

Because algum is also mentioned as a native of Lebanon (2 Ch 2.8), KB suggests that it is identical with Juniperus phoenicea excelsa 'which is excellent timber and abundantly to be found on Mount Lebanon'.

There is no valid reason for assuming that almug and algum are different trees.

REFERENCES: 1 K 10.11, 12; 2 Ch 2.8; 9.10, 11

Almond (*Amygdalus communis*)
a. flowering shoot
b. shoot with fruit   *c.* seed

Almond tree   Amygdalus communis

Hebrew: shaqedh, luz

DESCRIPTION: The almond tree belongs to the peach family. It grows wild in Palestine and Syria, reaching a height of 4.5 to 6 m. During the winter it sheds its leaves, which are oblong. The flowers, white or pink, bloom as early as January, appearing long before the leaves. This explains the Hb name for the tree, 'the wakeful' (see Je 1.11). The fruit is a drupe, i.e. a fleshy or pulpy fruit enclosing a stone, which in this case contains oil.

Ec 12.5 mentions the almond tree as a sign of the beauty of spring which does not bring joy to an old man.

Luz is also the name of a town in Ephraim, probably derived from the fact that the hills abounded with almond trees (Gn 28.19).

[89]

REFERENCES: shaqedh: Gn 43.11; Nu 17.8; Ec 12.5; Je 1.11
Luz: Gn 28.19; 30.37

DIFFICULT PASSAGES: Ex 25.33-34; 37.19-20: the Hb meshuq-qadhim is most likely a participial plural of a verb derived from shaqedh and is usually translated 'shaped like almonds', or (JB) 'like almond blossoms'.

Aloes   Aloë succotrina,   Aquilaria agallocha

Hebrew: ʔahalim, ʔahaloth   Greek: aloē

DESCRIPTION: Aloes is an aromatic substance mentioned in the Bible together with myrrh, balm and other fragrant plants, e.g. Ps 45.8; Pr 7.17; Jn 19.39.

Most modern commentators consider that these passages refer to two different plants. The plant mentioned in the OT is likely to have been Aquilaria agallocha, the eaglewood, a large tree which may reach a height of 36 m. It is native to south-east Asia and northern India. The tree secretes an aromatic resin, especially when it is old.

The aloē of John 19 is the Aloë succotrina, named after its native island, Socotra in the Indian Ocean, south of Arabia. Its thick succulent leaves form a tight rosette; the flowers are red and bell-shaped, growing together on a spike. The aromatic juice is extracted from the leaves. Although the fragrance is very pleasant, the taste is bitter. Like myrrh, aloes had to be imported into Israel, which made it expensive. The large quantity brought by Nicodemus, 'about a hundred pounds weight', is an indication of his wealth. The Aloë is a medicinal plant known from very early times and used by the Egyptians for embalming the dead.

REFERENCES: ʔahalim, ʔahaloth: Nu 24.6 (NEB 'lign-aloes');
Ps 45.8; Pr 7.17; SS 4.14
aloē: Jn 19.39

DIFFICULT PASSAGES: It may seem incongruous that Balaam's description of the landscape in Nu 24.6 includes mention of a tree which is not indigenous. But the words are not to be understood as an authentic portrait of the land of Canaan; he 'sees the vision of the Almighty'. SS 4.14 lists costly plants and trees which belong to the garden of a rich man who can afford to import them from foreign countries.

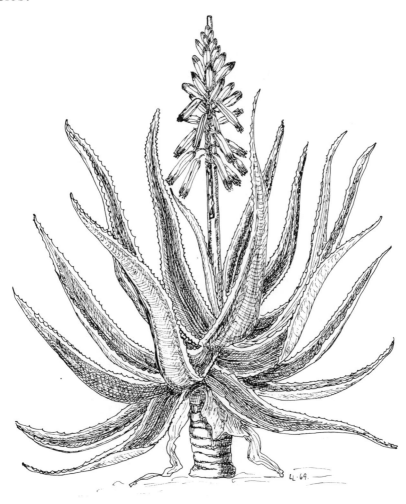

Aloes (*Alöe succotrina*)
flowering plant with stem shortened

Apricot (*Prunus armeniaca*)
a. flowering shoot
b. shoot with fruit   *c.* seed (stone)

Apricot, Apple   Prunus armeniaca

Hebrew: tappuaḥ

DESCRIPTION: The Hb word tappuaḥ has usually been rendered
'apple' (malus). The literal meaning of the word is 'a sweet-
smelling fruit or plant', as it is derived from a root napaḥ meaning
'to breathe or blow'.

While domesticated apple trees are now found in Palestine, Post,
quoted in Moldenke, definitely states that he has not seen any wild
specimens there, although wild apple trees are found in areas near
by. The fruit of the wild apple tree is not very attractive, being
both small and acid, so that it is extremely unlikely that tappuaḥ
should be translated 'apple'.

[92]

Authorities differ, but most modern botanists are inclined to identify tappuaḥ with the apricot, <u>Prunus armeniaca</u>, which does seem 'to meet all requirements of the context' (Tristram). It is abundant in Palestine, and most probably has been ever since Biblical times.

The tree is 9 m tall with reddish bark. Pink flowers appear before its heart-shaped leaves. Moldenke says that in Cyprus apricots are still known as 'golden apples' (cf Pr 25.11). NEB translates as 'apricot' in the Song of Solomon.

REFERENCES: Pr 25.11; SS 2.3, 5; 7.8; 8.5; Joel 1.12

OTHER PASSAGES: Dt 32.10; Ps 17.8; Pr 7.2; Zech 2.8; La 2.18 (AV). The 'apple of the eye' is English idiom for the Hb 'pupil of the eye', referring to anything extremely precious.

Balm   Balanites aegyptiaca,   Pistacia lentiscus

Hebrew: <u>tsori</u>

DESCRIPTION: RSV translates <u>tsori</u> as 'balm', but there has been and still is much uncertainty with regard to its identity.

Many commentators today follow Moldenke and ID in suggesting that in all passages except Gn 43.11 <u>tsori</u> should be identified with <u>Balanites aegyptiaca</u>, the 'Jericho balsam' which is common in the Jordan valley and the Dead Sea region.

<u>Balanites aegyptiaca</u> is found all over Egypt (as the name implies) as well as in Palestine. It is a desert plant, which grows into a tree 2.7 to 4.5 m tall with thorny branches, leathery and woolly leaves and green flowers. The fruits contain oil which is said to possess healing properties. Post identifies it with the 'balm of Gilead', <u>Commiphora opobalsamum</u>, and quotes Josephus who said that this plant was cultivated in the Jericho plain from the time of Solomon. Moldenke denies that <u>Commiphora opobalsamum</u> is native to Palestine and maintains that it is indigenous to Arabia. He adds that the way Gn 43.11 refers to <u>tsori</u> seems to imply an export of native products.

As Balanites aegyptiaca is native both to Egypt and Palestine, and Gn 43.11 implies that Jacob wants his sons to take something not found in Egypt, Moldenke suggests that tsori here may refer to the mastic tree, Pistacia lentiscus. This is denied, however, by ID, which retains Balanites aegyptiaca for the sake of consistency. It does not invariably follow that one Hb word always applies to the same plant. In this case tsori could refer to the gum or oil from more than one plant.

Pistacia lentiscus is a shrub or tree, 1 to 3 m tall, with ever-green leaves. The mastic or 'balm' is the gummy sap which exudes from the stem after incisions have been made.

See also MYRRH, SPICES, STACTE.

REFERENCES: Gn 37.25; 43.11; Je 8.22; 46.11; 51.8; Ezk 27.17

Balm (*Pistacia lentiscus*)
part of shoot, with fruit

[94]

Balm (*Balanites ægyptiaca*)
a. twig with flowers and leaves
b. part of thorny branch   *c*. flower   *d*. fruit

Barley Hordeum distichon

Hebrew: se'orah   Greek: krithē

DESCRIPTION: A description of barley is not necessary as it is one of the oldest cultivated plants. It was grown in Egypt in 5000 BC and is cultivated today over most of the Northern hemisphere. Barley grows well in both warm and cold temperatures and in dry and damp climates.

It is interesting to note the prices of wheat and barley in the description of the famine during the siege of Samaria (2 K 7.1). Ordinary food was very expensive, but wheat cost twice as much as barley, the cheapest food obtainable. Used mainly for feeding cattle, barley also served for making bread in times of emergency, as in Samaria during the siege, and among the poor (2 S 17.28; Ezk 4.9; Rv 6.6).

The low cost of barley makes it a symbol of disparagement (Ho 3.2; Nu 5.15; Ezk 13.19). 'A cake of barley' in Jg 7.13 is a derogatory term for an Israelite, just as 'tent' stands for the Bedouin.

The barley harvest comes early, in the lower regions of Palestine in March-April, in the mountains in May, a month earlier than wheat (Ex 9.31). It was therefore often necessary to eat barley cakes early in the year (2 K 4.42). So, for example, it does not necessarily imply poverty when Jesus feeds 5000 people with five barley loaves (Jn 6.9). This was early in the year, before the Passover (v 4).

REFERENCES: se'orah: Consult a concordance
krithē: Rv 6.6
krithinos ('made of barley'): Jn 6.9, 13

Bdellium   Commiphora (Africana)

Hebrew: bedholaḥ

DESCRIPTION: Most modern commentators follow the oldest tradition according to which the Hb word is explained as referring to bdellium, a yellowish transparent and fragrant gum which flows out from an incision in the bark of a certain shrub, probably some species of Commiphora (perhaps Africana), which grows in South Arabia.

The meaning 'bdellium' is, however, doubtful. According to a later tradition it was understood to be a pearl or some precious stone.

REFERENCES: Gn 2.12; Nu 11.7

Bean Vicia faba

Hebrew: pol

DESCRIPTION: The broad bean has been known as food since the Bronze Age (3000-2000 BC). It is an annual plant which reaches a height of 60 to 90 cm. The small oval leaves are greyish-green; the flowers, situated in the axils between branch and leaf, are white with a purplish blotch. The pods are large and contain the brown compressed seeds.

The crop ripens at the time of wheat harvest. Beans are grown in gardens and in the fields. They constitute a nourishing food and are eaten either boiled or roasted. Sometimes they are mixed with grain flour for bread-making.

REFERENCES: 2 S 17.28; Ezk 4.9

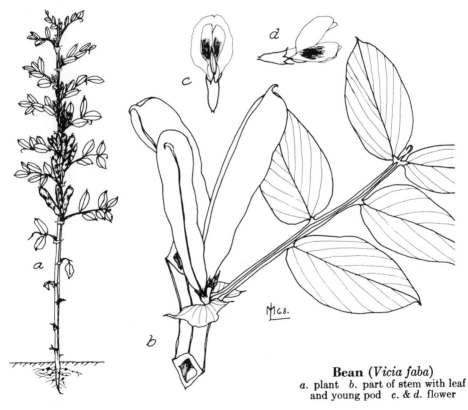

Bean (*Vicia faba*)
a. plant *b.* part of stem with leaf
and young pod *c. & d.* flower

Bitter herbs Centaurea

Hebrew: merorim

DESCRIPTION: The Hb word means 'bitter'. In the two passages mentioned below, it is used in connection with instructions for the passover meal, and is translated as 'bitter herbs' in most versions. Some modern scholars identify this herb with the Centaurea, of which several species are found in the desert areas of Palestine. It has small flower heads protected by thorns, and its leaves grow in rosettes and are bitter in taste. Even now the Bedouin eat them as salad.

Moldenke and others are more inclined to suppose that the merorim were plants like endive (Cichorium endivia), chicory (Cichorium intybus), dandelion (Taraxacum officinale), and sorrel (Rumex acetocella).

REFERENCES: Ex 12.8;
Nu 9.11

Bitter herbs (*Cichorium intybus*)

[98]

Bitter herbs (*Taraxacum vulgare*)

Box tree Buxus longifolia

Hebrew: te?ashshur

DESCRIPTION: The long-leaved box is an evergreen shrub or tree with oblong leaves. The rather slender stem may attain a height of 6 m. The wood is very hard and suitable for carpentry and wood-carving. Post (and Walker) have found it growing in the mountain-ous regions of Palestine. Some botanists therefore are inclined to identify te?ashshur with the box tree. RSV translates 'pine', JB 'cypress', 'box' or 'cedar'. See also CYPRESS. (See page 100 for illustration of box tree.)

REFERENCES: Is 41.19; 60.13; Ezk 27.6

[99]

Broom Retama raetam

Hebrew: rothem

DESCRIPTION: Most modern commentators are of the opinion that
the word rothem stands for the broom, Arabic ratam, which grows in
the deserts of Palestine and Arabia.   It is a bush with many branches
and twigs, a few small leaves, and large clusters of white flowers.
Its wood, together with the large stem of the root, is used by the
Bedouin for making charcoal (see JB and NEB of Ps 120.4: 'red-hot
charcoal').   AV and RV translate 'juniper'.

REFERENCES: 1 K 19.4, 5 (JB 'furze'); Job 30.4; Ps 120.4

DIFFICULT PASSAGE: Job 30.4: Moldenke points out that the root
of broom is poisonous, and identifies the plant with the scarlet

4.69

Box tree (*Buxus longifolia*)

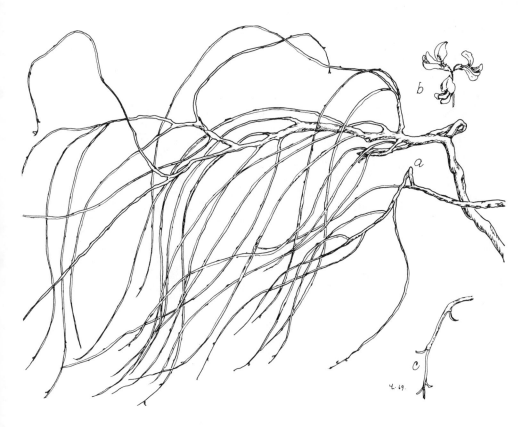

Broom (*Retama rœtam*)
a. branches *b*. inflorescence
c. tip of branch

Cynomorium. Moffatt and Fohrer conjecture leḥummam 'for giving warmth', instead of laḥmam 'for their food'. So also RV mg
and RSV. But the point of the verse could be that these refugees to
the desert are so hungry and starved that they are glad to eat anything. In which case, retain 'their food', with JB and NEB. LXX
keeps this idea, though greatly expanding the verse: 'Who encircle
saltworts with loud cries, whose food was saltworts, who were
without honour and of no repute, and who chewed the roots of trees
because of great hunger.'

[101]

Caper plant capparis spinosa, c. sicula

Hebrew: ʔabhiyonah

DESCRIPTION: The caper plant grows everywhere in Palestine, Syria and Lebanon. Its heavy, drooping branches cover the walls of Jerusalem and the rocks of many valleys. It blooms in May, and its large white flowers are open for only one night. The buds are pickled in vinegar and eaten as a condiment with meat. Both fruit and buds are supposed to stimulate appetite. In ancient times caper-berries were also said to stimulate sexual desire.

ʔabhiyonah, rendered 'desire' in AV and RSV, is identified in modern dictionaries with the caper berry (so also JB and NEB). This accords with the LXX (kapparis) and Vulgate (capparis), as well as with the botanists Löw, Post and Moldenke.

The accompanying verb tapher (from parar 'to break') is translated either 'to fail' or 'to burst', thus illustrating the failing powers of an old man, his loss of taste and appetite.

REFERENCE: Ec 12.5

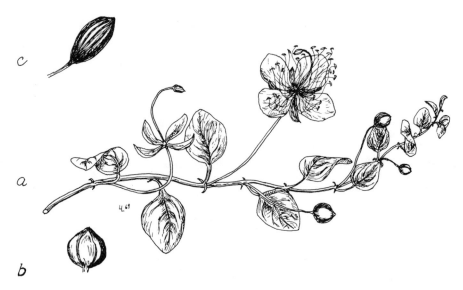

Caper plant (*Capparis spinosa*)
a. flowering shoot   *b.* bud   *c.* fruit

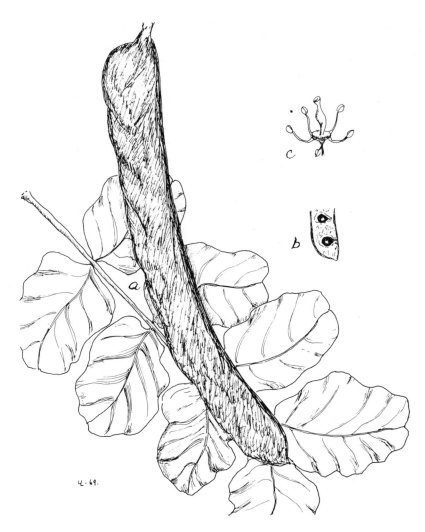

Carob (*Ceratonia siliqua*)
a. leaf and fruit   *b.* half of fruit with seed
c. flower showing style and stamens

Carob tree   Ceratonia siliqua

Greek: keration

DESCRIPTION: The Gk word keration literally means 'a little horn', and only occurs once in the NT, in the parable of the Prodigal Son, where it stands for the 'pods' or 'husks' generally eaten by pigs. The pod of the carob tree is shaped like a little horn, from 15 to 25 cm long and 2.5 to 3.7 cm broad; when ripe it has a rich content of syrup which makes it a valuable and nourishing food for cattle and pigs. Now, as in the past, the fruit of the carob tree is also eaten by poor people.

The carob tree is grown in almost all Mediterranean countries and has been introduced into America. It is an evergreen tree reaching a height of 9 m. The leaves resemble those of the ash tree. The flowers are small, yellow or red, and the fruits ripen in April and May.

The carob tree is sometimes called 'St. John's bread tree' because it has been assumed that the honey eaten by John the Baptist in the desert was not real honey but the syrup pressed out of the pod of the carob tree. It is also sometimes called 'locust tree' because some commentators mistakenly assume that the locusts mentioned in Mt 3.4 were not real insects but the fruits of the carob tree. See LOCUST.

REFERENCE: Lk 15.16

Cassia   Cinnamomum cassia, Saussurea lappa

Hebrew: qiddah, qetsi'oth

DESCRIPTION: The derivation of the Hb word qiddah as well as its identification is dubious, although some have tried to explain it as meaning 'a bark that peels off'. The context denotes an aromatic plant, and an old tradition identifies this with cassia, a tree native to Ceylon and India, and much like the cinnamon tree. The thick coarse bark is used as a spice when peeled off and dried, although it is inferior to cinnamon. The buds may also be added to food as seasoning. The smaller leaves and pods are sometimes used for medicinal purposes.

The plant bears no relation to the Linnaean genus Cassia, which includes the sennas.

AV, RV and RSV transliterate the Hb word qetsi'oth in Ps 45.8 as 'cassia'. JB 'myrrh and aloes waft from your robes'; NEB 'your

robes are all fragrant with myrrh and powder of aloes'. Some commentators, quoted in Moldenke, suggest that David and Solomon
could have known the Indian orris, Saussurea lappa. This native
of the Himalayas is a perennial with large leaves, a prickly stem
and purple flowers. Its roots are strongly aromatic and can be used
for perfumes and incense.

REFERENCES: qiddah: Ex 30.24; Ezk 27.19
            qetsi'oth: Ps 45.8

Cassia (*Saussurea lappa*)
leaves and inflorescence

Castor oil plant (*Ricinus communis*)
a. shoot with flowers *b.* inflorescence (female
flowers above, male below) *c.* mature fruit *d.* seed

Castor oil plant   Ricinus communis

Hebrew: qiqayon

DESCRIPTION: There have been different opinions with regard to
the translation of the Hb qiqayon. The Vulgate translates as 'ivy';
AV and NEB follow the LXX in translating as 'gourd'. In the Orient
the gourd, Cucurbita pepo (pumpkin) develops a rapid growth with
the possibility of giving shade, as the book of Jonah vividly describes.

Most modern botanists (e. g. Moldenke) and interpreters (e. g.
T. H. Robinson) have adopted a suggestion made by Jerome, trans-

lator of the Vulgate, that qiqayon might be the castor oil tree, Ricinus communis or Palma Christi. This is a fast-growing plant which can reach a height of 3 m. Its leaves are large and well-suited for providing shelter or shade. Its fruits are capsules with three seeds containing oil. As well as these features, another reason for identifying qiqayon with Ricinus communis is the similarity between the Hb word and the Egyptian kiki and Assyrian kukanitu. JB and NEB mg translate as 'castor oil plant'.

REFERENCES: Jon 4.6, 7, 9, 10

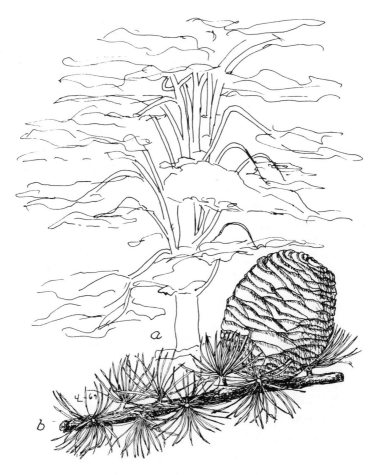

Cedar (*Cedrus libani*)
a. outline of tree   *b*. branch with cone

Cedar   Cedrus libani

Hebrew: ʔerez

DESCRIPTION: The enthusiasm with which the OT writings praise the cedar of Lebanon is understandable. It is a majestic tree of great beauty, reaching 27 m in height and 12 m in girth. Its long branches spread out horizontally from the trunk, and the leaves are dark and evergreen, glittering like silver in the sun. The cones take three years to mature. The fragrant wood is much sought after for building purposes, as it does not easily rot. Its great value as timber is often mentioned, especially in the history of King Solomon.

REFERENCES: Consult a concordance

DIFFICULT PASSAGES: Lv 14.4-6 and 49-52; Nu 19.6. Although most commentators, including the modern ones, translate ʔerez in these passages as 'cedar wood', it is understood by some scholars to be a different kind of cedar, or a juniper. Walker identifies it with Juniperus oxycedrus, other scholars with Sabina phoenicia, which grows in the Sinai mountains. Cedars of Lebanon were never common outside Lebanon, and in these passages some easily available aromatic wood seems to be implied.

Is 44.14: RSV, JB and NEB translate ʔoren as 'cedar'; on this see LAUREL.

Cinnamon   Cinnamomum zeylanicum

Hebrew: qinnamon   Greek: kinnamōmon

DESCRIPTION: This evergreen tree, belonging to the Laurel family, is a native of Ceylon and Malaya. It grows to 9 m high and is cultivated for its valuable inner bark, from which the cinnamon is obtained. The bark is cut and then easily peeled off. Cinnamon was used as a condiment because of its delicious flavour; also as a perfume and an ingredient of 'holy' oil.

REFERENCES: qinnamon: Ex 30.23; Pr 7.17 (NEB 'cassia'); SS 4.14
kinnamōmon: Rv 18.13

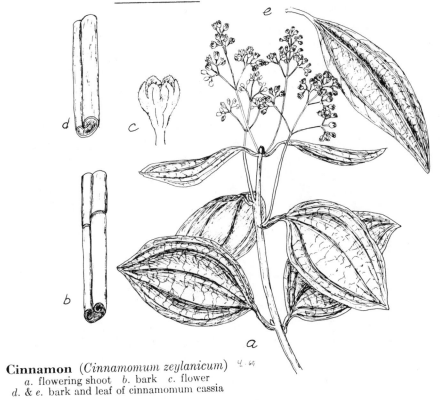

Cinnamon (*Cinnamomum zeylanicum*) 4.69
  a. flowering shoot *b.* bark *c.* flower
d. & *e.* bark and leaf of cinnamomum cassia

Citron tree, Sandarac tree Tetraclinis articulata (or Thuja arti-
culata)

Greek: thuinos (literally: 'from the citron tree')

DESCRIPTION: The citron tree, a conifer belonging to the cypress
family, is a tree or shrub about 9 m high, with reddish-brown bark
and spreading or ascending branches. Its bright-green leaves are
very small and scaly. The tree has always been highly valued for
its fragrant wood which takes on a fine dark polish, and it was said
to be worth its weight in gold. The wood is durable, usually resisting all attacks by insects. The tree is a native of Morocco, the
Atlas mountains and Algeria. It is not related to the Citrus or
orange.

[109]

DIFFICULT PASSAGE: Moldenke (and Post) seem to have dispelled all doubt about the identification of <u>xulon thuinon</u>, rendering it 'Sandarac tree'. RSV and NEB say 'scented wood'; AV transliterates 'thyine wood'. The Zürich Bible has 'wohlriechendes Holz' and Menge 'Thujaholz', as does Danish and JB (French). JB (English) has 'sandalwood'.

Coriander (*Coriandrum sativum*)
a. plant   *b.* fruit   *c.* fruiting head
d. central floret   *e.* outside floret   *f.* leaf

Coriander   Coriandrum sativum

Hebrew: <u>gadh</u>

DESCRIPTION: Coriander is mentioned only twice in the Bible, to illustrate what manna was like.

Coriander is well known in Palestine. It is an annual umbelliferous plant like the carrot, 61 cm high, with divided leaves and umbels of pink or white flowers. The plant has a strong characteristic odour. Its fruit or seeds are grey, globular and the size of a small pea. They are used as a spice in cooking, and the aromatic oil derived from the seeds is used in perfume.

REFERENCES: Ex 16.31; Nu 11.7

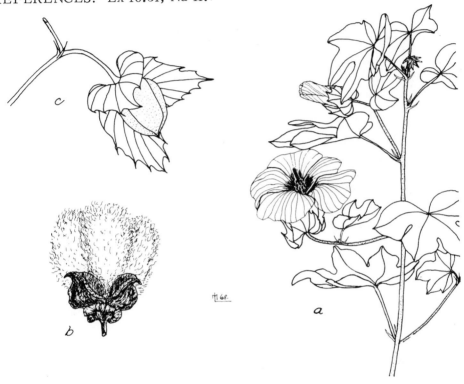

Cotton (*Gossypium herbaceum*)
a. plant *b.* mature capsule, open
c. unripe fruit, with bracts

Cotton, Levant Cotton Gossypium herbaceum

Hebrew: karpas

DESCRIPTION: Cotton is an annual plant, growing into a bush about 1.5 m high, with yellow or pink flowers and deeply-lobed leaves. Its fruit is a capsule with several seeds densely covered with long white fluffy hairs.

Cotton is mentioned only in Es 1.6, in a vivid description of the sumptuous feast held by the Persian king in his winter residence in Susa. The author takes pains to describe the magnificent decorations of the courtyard in front of the palace: 'There were white cotton curtains and blue hangings caught up with cords...' (RSV), probably so that they could serve as an awning. AV and RV (but not RV mg) mistakenly translate karpas as 'green'. JB has 'white and violet hangings', and NEB 'white curtains'. Cotton has been cultivated in Persia from ancient times, and tree cotton, Gossypium arboreum, is mentioned in the cuneiform inscriptions of Sennacherib.

Although the Greek traveller and writer Pausanias (2nd century AD) describes Judaean cotton, some modern botanists doubt that it was cultivated in Palestine in Biblical times. However, Pausanias' statement is supported by the Mishna (the written doctrines of the Jewish rabbis from the 3rd century AD).

The Hb word ḥur literally means 'a white material' (of linen or cotton). It appears only in Es 1.6 and 8.15. In Es 1.6 it is natural to connect the word with the following karpas and translate 'white cotton'.

There is no real justification for the note 'or cotton' in RV mg of Gn 41.42.

REFERENCE: Es 1.6

Cucumber Cucumis chate (Cucumis melo)

Hebrew: qishshu?

DESCRIPTION: A fruit which was grown in Egypt in Biblical times and is mentioned in Nu 11.5. It was natural that throughout the heat of the desert journey the children of Israel were longing for the refreshment of the Cucumis chate, which is larger, sweeter and more watery and melon-like than the ordinary European cucumber

(Cucumis sativus). Even today a cucumber and a piece of bread often make up a meal in Egypt.

There seems, however, to be some doubt whether the qishshu? should be identified with Cucumis chate or with Cucumis melo, the muskmelon, as ID says.

REFERENCES: Nu 11.5. A cucumber or melon field, miqshah, is mentioned in Is 1.8; Je 10.5.

DIFFICULT PASSAGE: Je 10.5: Gesenius derives miqshah from q-sh-h and translates 'hammered work', 'statue'. Most modern commentators translate 'cucumber field', so RSV and RV mg. JB 'melon patch', NEB 'plot of cucumbers'. AV 'upright as a palm tree', followed by RV, may be ignored.

Cucumber (*Cucumis chate* [*melo*])
a. fruit and leaves
b. flower (male)   *c.* bud (female)

b   a

4.69.

Cummin (*Cuminum cyminum*)
a. plant with fruiting head   *b.* fruit

Cummin   Cuminum cyminum

Hebrew: kammon   Greek: kuminon

DESCRIPTION: This is an annual plant of the carrot family, native
to Mediterranean countries, 30 to 60 cm high and bearing umbels
of small white flowers.   It is cultivated for its seeds, which are
used as a spice, for instance in bread.   Isaiah (28.25, 27) gives a
vivid description of how cummin is sown and harvested; when ripe it
is beaten with a rod.

Dt 14.22 and Mishna ('All which serves as food and grows out of the field must be tithed') stress the duty of tithing even the smallest fruits. The words of Jesus to the Pharisees in Mt 23.23 refer to this. See also DILL.

REFERENCES: kammon: Is 28.25, 27
                  kuminon: Mt 23.23

Cypress Cupressus sempervirens horizontalis

Hebrew: te'ashshur

DESCRIPTION: There is much disagreement as to the rendering of te'ashshur. Some (e.g. BDB, Moldenke, AV, RV and NEB) translate 'the box tree' (Buxus longifolia), found formerly in the Galilean hills, northern Palestine and Lebanon.

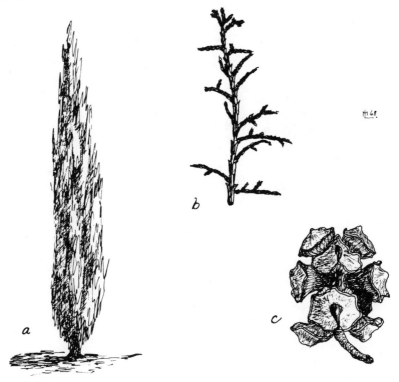

Cypress (*Cupressus sempervirens*)
a. outline of tree   *b.* twig   *c.* ripe cone

Others identify it with some kind of conifer or cedar. RSV usually translates te?ashshur as 'pine' and berosh as 'cypress'. See PINE (ALEPPO PINE).

There is great confusion in all versions, ancient and modern, over the identity of evergreens in the Bible. We follow ID which identifies te?ashshur with Cupressus sempervirens horizontalis, as does Fohrer and also RV mg. The cypress is native to Palestine and is found growing wild in Gilead and Edom at the present day. It is an evergreen, 9 to 15 m high, with spreading branches, small scale-like leaves and round cones. The durability of the wood makes it suitable for building purposes.

AV and JB translate tirzah in Is 44.14 as 'cypress'; RV and RSV 'holm tree' (q.v.)

REFERENCES: Is 41.19; 60.13; Ezk 27.6

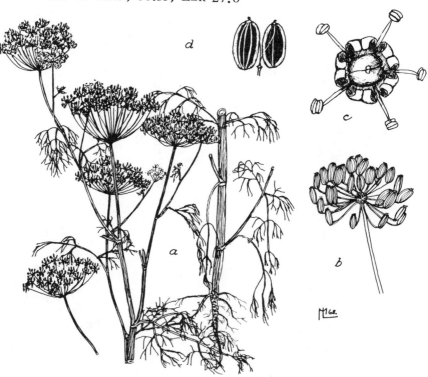

Dill (*Anethum graveolens*)
a. plant *b.* fruiting head *c.* flowers *d.* mature split fruit

Dill   Anethum graveolens

Greek: anēthon

DESCRIPTION: Dill is an annual umbelliferous plant, 30 to 50 cm
high with yellow flowers. It is quite common in Palestine, both wild
and cultivated, and is grown for its seeds which contain aromatic
oils used as a seasoning.

AV renders anēthon as 'anise', Phillips as 'aniseed'. The
Jubilee Bible even adds an illustration of this plant (which has some
resemblance to dill). Moldenke however does not question its identification as 'dill', and he is supported by Strack-Billerbeck.

Some translations, including RSV and NEB, render the Hb word
qetsaḥ in Is 28.25, 27 as 'dill'. JB has 'fennel'. But according to
Post, Moldenke, Gesenius, and Buhl, qetsaḥ is to be understood as
black cummin, Nigella sativa, and kammon as cummin, Cuminum
cyminum. See CUMMIN and NUTMEG.

REFERENCE: Mt 23.23

Ebony Diospyros ebenum

Hebrew: hobhnim

DESCRIPTION: The three species of Diospyros: ebenaster, mela-
noxylon and ebenum, the so-called 'date-trees', are natives of India
and Ceylon. They are large slow-growing trees with a smooth bark,
leaves nearly 10 cm long, and small bell-shaped pink flowers. It
is the heartwood of this tree which makes it valuable. It is black
and very hard, and has been used by woodcarvers since antiquity.
Together with ivory, it is used for inlaying and ornamental turnery.

REFERENCE: Ezk 27.15

DIFFICULT PASSAGE: For the rendering of geographical names in
this passage, see OTTP, p 207.

Fig tree, Fig   *Ficus carica*

Hebrew: te?enah (fig and fig tree), pag (early fig), bikkurah (early fig), debhelah (pressed fig cake)

Greek: sukē (fig tree), sukon (fig), olunthos (late fig)

DESCRIPTION: The fig tree is a native of Western Asia, but was and still is much cultivated in Palestine. Together with the vine and the olive tree, it constituted the most important and useful fruit tree of the Israelites. If the ground is well cultivated and the tree taken care of, it will reward its owner with two abundant harvests every year. The early figs ripen in June, the late ones in August and September. The late figs are often pressed into cakes and thus preserved for export.

The fig tree grows to a height of 6 m and has long curved branches, which sometimes give it the appearance of a large bush. Its trunk and branches are smooth; the bark is silver-grey in colour. The leaves are large and shaped like a hand, and the thick foliage affords a pleasant shade (see e.g. Jn 1.48).

The fruit is a well-known and popular delicacy in many parts of the world, and is very nourishing because of its high sugar content. It is also used medicinally (2 K 20.7). Early figs are chiefly appreciated for their fine flavour.

4.69.

Ebony (*Diospyros ebenum*)

4.69.

Fig (*Ficus carica*)

REFERENCES: te?enah: Consult a concordance
pag: SS 2.13
debhelah: 1 S 25.18; 30.12; 2 K 20.7; 1 Ch 12.40;
  Is 38.21
bikkurah: Is 28.4; Je 24.2; Ho 9.10; Mi 7.1
sukē: Mt 21.19-21; 24.32; Mk 11.13, 20f; 13.28; Lk
  13.6f; 21.29; Jn 1.48, 50; Jas 3.12; Rv 6.13
sukon: Mt 7.16; Mk 11.13; Lk 6.44; Jas 3.12
olunthos: Rv 6.13

Flax Linum usitatissimum

Hebrew: pesheth, pishtah

Greek: linon, bussos, sindōn, othonia

DESCRIPTION: Flax is one of the oldest cultivated plants, and may
have been known for four to five thousand years. Its original native
soil is unknown, but it was probably in Mesopotamia. The cultivation of flax in ancient Palestine is attested by the Talmud.

[119]

It grows nearly one m high, with small narrow leaves, and its flowers have five bright blue petals. The fruit is a capsule; the seeds contain an oil which is used as food and in the paint industry. After the harvest, formerly carried out by pulling up the crop with its root, the stalks were spread on the flat roofs of the houses to dry in the sun. Then they were split and combed until the fibres could be separated and peeled off. These were woven into linen.

The Hb and Gk words stand both for the plant, flax, and for linen. Pishtah and linon can also mean 'wick'. In the NT the fabric and the wick are mentioned, but not the plant. Othonia is translated 'linen clothes', 'linen cloths', 'strips of linen cloth' by AV, RSV, JB and NEB. The Gk word is probably from ʔeṭun of Pr 7.16.

REFERENCES: pesheth, pishtah: Ex 9.31; Jos 2.6; Jg 15.14; Pr 31.13; Is 19.9; 42.3; Ezk 40.3; Ho 2.5, 9

Flax (*Linum usitatissimum*)
a. flowering plant   b. mature capsule   c. seed

linon: Mt 12.20 (cf Is 42.3); Rv 15.6
sindōn: Mt 27.59; Mk 15.46; Lk 23.53.   In Mk
  14.51f it should be translated 'tunic'.
othonia: Jn 19.40; 20.5, 7
bussos: Lk 16.19

Frankincense   Boswellia

Hebrew: lebonah   Greek: libanos

DESCRIPTION: Frankincense is a balsamic gum exuding from the
wood of different species of shrubs and trees belonging to the genus
Boswellia.   The bark is incised, and the finest quality of resin is

Frankincense (*Boswellia carterii*)
a. branch with leaves and flowers   *b.* flower

[121]

obtained if this is done not too early in the year. The different spe-cies of Boswellia are native to India, the Somali coast and Arabia; the Midianites imported frankincense from Ephah and Sheba, Is 60.6; Je 6.20. Whether the Boswellia was grown in Palestine is rather doubtful. The 'hill of frankincense' mentioned in SS 4.6 and the place name in Jg 21.19 do not prove this.

Frankincense was used in the offerings in the temple and was an ingredient of the holy ointment.

REFERENCES: lebonah: Consult a concordance
libanos: Mt 2.11; Rv 18.13

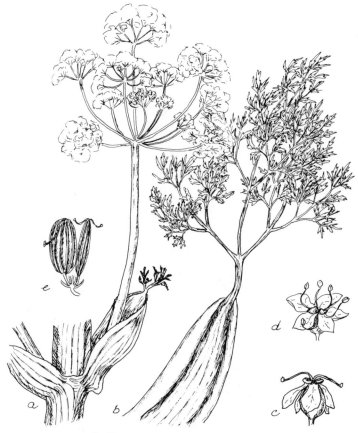

Galbanum (*Ferula galbaniflua*)
a. part of flowering plant *b.* leaf with part of swollen stalk
c. flower (female) *d.* flower (male) *e.* seeds

[122]

Galbanum Ferula galbaniflua

Hebrew: ḥelbenah

DESCRIPTION: Galbanum is a kind of fragrant resin which comes from the Ferula galbaniflua, an umbelliferous member of the carrot family, a perennial with a strong tap root and a stem one m or more high. Its leaves are deeply cut and its greenish-white flowers are arranged in umbels. When ripe the young stem yields a milky juice if it is cut a few inches above the ground. The resinous gum soon solidifies and changes to an amber colour. If burnt it gives off a very pleasant odour. Galbanum is a native of Persia. In Biblical times it was imported into Palestine, where it was used as an ingredient of the holy incense. See also MYRRH.

REFERENCE: Ex 30.34

Gopher Cupressus sempervirens (?)

Hebrew: gopher

DESCRIPTION: The Hb word occurs only once in the Bible, in connection with the building of Noah's ark. It is still an open question what kind of material is meant. Some translators and commentators therefore prefer simply to render 'gopher wood', even without any explanatory notes (e. g. RSV and 'Our Living Bible').

Others (e. g. NEB) derive it from a root parallel to the Gk kuparissos, cypress, which seems likely as the Phoenicians used this kind of wood for shipbuilding. It has also been pointed out that the word is similar to Aramaic and Assyrian words meaning 'bitumen'. Finally, some commentators consider it to be a misspelling of a word meaning 'brimstone', or some foreign word indicating a kind of pine-wood (JB 'resinous wood').

Because of the word 'ets ('tree, wood') with which it is connected, it seems some kind of pine tree is implied.

REFERENCE: Gn 6.14

Gourd *(Citrullus colocynthis)*
a. shoot with flowers and leaves   *b.* male flower opened
c. female flower cut through

Gourd Citrullus colocynthis

Hebrew: paqqu'oth

DESCRIPTION: There is little doubt about the identification of this plant, the characteristics of which are so vividly described in 2 K 4. The Hb name is derived from a root p-q-' meaning 'to split' or 'to burst', which describes the fruit's habit of bursting when ripe.

The wild gourd resembles the cucumber, with its stem trailing along the ground. Its leaves are deep-cut, shaped rather like those of the vine. When ripe the fruit is dried to a powder which is used medicinally for its strong purgative qualities. NEB translates paqqu'oth as 'bitter-apples'.

For 'gourd' in Jon 4.6ff see CASTOR OIL PLANT.

REFERENCE: 2 K 4.39

DIFFICULT PASSAGES: 1 K 6.18; 7.24: peqa'im 'gourd-shaped', referring to the carved ornaments in the temple.

Grass, Herb, Hay   Gramineæ (Butomus umbellatus)

Hebrew: hatsir, ?ahu, deshe?, hashash, 'esebh

Greek: chortos, botanē, lachanon

DESCRIPTION: Gramineæ is the botanical name which comprises the whole grass family. A botanist travelling in Palestine has identified 460 different grasses, so that in most cases it will be impossible to know which of them is mentioned in the different Scripture passages. An exception is ?ahu, said to be an Egyptian word and often identified with a plant growing on the borders of the Nile, with papyrus. Moldenke suggests that this is Butomus umbellatus. RSV and NEB translate 'reed grass' or 'reed'; JB 'rush'.

In other connections the word 'grass' is used symbolically in the Bible (e.g. in Ps 90 and Is 40) and by Jesus when he talks about the grass that withers during the drought as an illustration of human life and worldly glory.

The Gk word chortos means grass in the field, or wild grass in contrast to cultivated plants. In 1 Co 3.12 it means hay as building material.

botanē, originally a generic word signifying 'herb', 'plant' or 'fodder', should be rendered 'grass' or 'useful vegetation' in Hb 6.7.

lachanon is another generic word meaning 'edible garden herb', 'vegetable'. In Ro 14.2 it is used in describing persons who are weak in their convictions.

REFERENCES: hatsir: Consult a concordance
  ?ahu: Gn 41.2,18; Job 8.11 (Ho 13.15)
  deshe?: Gn 1.11,12; Dt 32.2; 2 S 23.4; 2 K 19.26;
    Job 6.5; 38.27; Ps 23.2; 37.2; Pr 27.25; Is 15.6;
    37.27; 66.14; Je 14.5
  hashash: Is 5.24; 33.11
  'esebh: Consult a concordance

chortos: Mt 6.30; 14.19; Mk 6.39; Lk 12.28; Jn 6.10;
   1 Co 3.12; Jas 1.10, 11; 1 P 1.24; Rv 8.7; 9.4
botanē: Hb 6.7
lachanon: Mt 13.32; Mk 4.32; Lk 11.42; Ro 14.2

DIFFICULT PASSAGES: Ho 13.15: The Hb text is difficult and probably corrupt, and the context suggests an emendation as in RSV,
'Though he may flourish as the reed plant', instead of 'though he
may flourish among brothers'.

   hatsir in Nu 11.5 is to be rendered 'leek' (see ONION, GARLIC,
LEEK).

Grass (*Butomus umbellatus*)
flower and upper part of leaves

Henna Lawsonia inermis

Hebrew: kopher

DESCRIPTION: AV renders the Hb word 'camphire'. But camphire or camphor is a plant native to China, not likely to have been known in Palestine in Biblical times.

The botanists Löw, Post and Moldenke identify the word with the henna plant, Lawsonia inermis, probably a native of India, which grows wild and is also cultivated in the warmer regions of Palestine, such as Jericho, Jaffa, and the oasis of Engedi (SS 1.14) on the shores of the Dead Sea.

Henna (*Lawsonia inermis*)
a. flowering shoot   *b.* shoot with fruits

[127]

This is a small tree with light green spear-shaped leaves, thorny branches and sweet-smelling flowers which grow in clusters. It used to be customary among wealthy women to wear a little bag filled with the aromatic henna flowers.

The leaves contain a dye which was used as a cosmetic in ancient Egypt, as it is today among the Arabs, for colouring the finger-nails and toe-nails. Whether this was a custom among the Israelites is not known for certain. Dt 21.10-14, where disapproval of the foreigners' use of cosmetics is implied, may refer to this practice.

The dye is prepared by mixing dried and crushed henna leaves with warm water.

REFERENCES: SS 1.14; 4.13 (7.11)

DIFFICULT PASSAGE: SS 7.11: See OTTP, p 137. Rudolph speaks in support of the translation 'henna bushes' (RSV and JB 'villages').

Holm Oak Quercus ilex

Hebrew: tirzah

DESCRIPTION: A commentator confronted with an unknown word like tirzah, which appears only once in the OT, is tempted to suppose that there has been a slip of the pen. Some therefore read tidhhar: see PINE (BRUTIAN PINE). Most commentators today follow the rendering of the Vulgate and translate 'ilex' or, like RSV and NEB, 'holm tree', though the identification is doubtful. JB has 'cypress'.

The Quercus ilex is a beautiful tree, which can reach a height of 15 m. It is a native of Mediterranean countries where it is often found growing on the coast or in the mountains, as it likes firm dry ground where its long roots can reach into the soil. Its oblong leaves are leathery and evergreen, smooth and shiny on the surface and lighter underneath. Its fruit is an acorn. When not cultivated, this tree usually grows alone.

Post identifies it with the <u>Pinus halepensis</u>: see PINE (ALEPPO PINE).

REFERENCE: Is 44.14

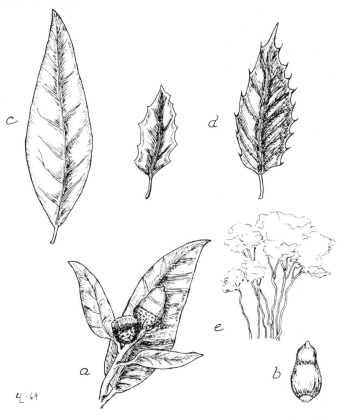

Holm oak (*Quercus ilex*)
a. twig with fruit   *b.* acorn
c. & d. different forms of leaves   *e.* group of trees

Hyssop   <u>Origanum maru</u>

Hebrew: <u>?ezobh</u>   Greek: <u>hussōpos</u>

DESCRIPTION: A plant with a shrub-like base and stems which are erect, stiff and strong.   When it grows from the ground it reaches a height of just under one m.   It may also spring out of crevices in walls, cliffs and rocks.   Its leaves and branches are hairy, and its

[129]

flowers white. The plant is aromatic, and the dried leaves are used as a condiment in Palestine and Egypt, where it grows. It belongs to the mint family. The leaves and little branches, when collected in bunches, were suitable for sprinkling purposes, as the hairy surface would hold the liquid. For this reason the plant was used in the ritual purifications of the Jews. In 1 Kings 4.33 it is a symbol of humility over against the majesty of the cedars of Lebanon.

NEB usually translates ʔezobh as 'marjoram'.

REFERENCES: ʔezobh: Ex 12.22; Lv 14.4, 6, 49, 51, 52; Nu 19.6, 18; 1 K 4.33; Ps 51.7
hussōpos: Jn 19.29; Hb 9.19

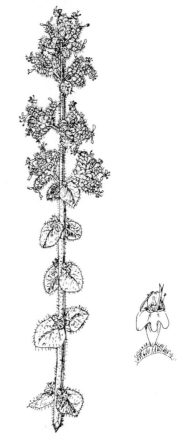

DIFFICULT PASSAGE: Jn 19.29. It has often been considered that the reed (Mk 15.36) to which the sponge was fastened would need to have been longer than the ordinary stem of origanum. This difficulty was felt by Moldenke, who suggests that the plant mentioned here should be understood as sorghum vulgare. An old conjecture substitutes hussō for hussōpō. This reading (found in one 11th-century minuscule) has been followed by the NEB translators: 'they soaked a sponge with the wine, fixed it on a javelin...'. But if the crucified was raised only 1.8 m from the ground, his mouth could be reached by means of a stem of origanum.

Hyssop (*Origanum maru*)
a. upper half of flowering plant *b.* flower

[130]

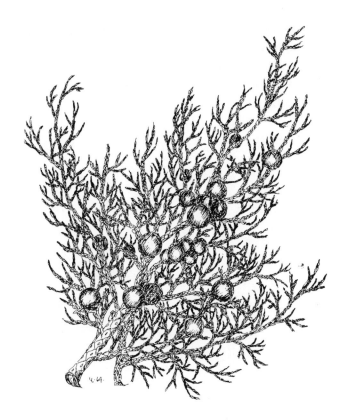

Juniper (*Juniperus phœnicia*)
branch with fruit

Juniper   Juniperus phoenicia

Hebrew: 'ar'ar, 'aro'er

DESCRIPTION: It is not clear which tree is meant by the Hb words. RSV simply says 'shrub' and JB 'scrub', while AV translates 'heath'. The heath tree, however, does not grow in the Palestinian deserts. ID (followed by NEB) suggests Juniperus phoenicia, which is found both singly and in groups in the deserts of Sinai and Edom. 'ar'ar is still the Arabic name for this shrub.

It is a shrub or small tree with minute leaves like scales, and small round tawny-coloured cones; it grows in the countries around the Mediterranean sea.

[131]

In Ps 102.17 the translation 'a naked man', i.e. a lonely or des-
titute man, has been suggested for 'ar'ar. Moldenke is more inclined to identify this with Juniperus oxycedrus. AV and RV translate rothem as 'juniper'. See BROOM. JB translates berosh as
'juniper' in some places. See PINE (ALEPPO PINE).

REFERENCES: Je 17.6; 48.6

DIFFICULT PASSAGE: For Je 48.6 see OTTP, p 179.

Laurel (*Laurus nobilis*)
a. with flowers   *b.* with fruits

Laurel, Sweet Bay   Laurus nobilis

Hebrew: ʔezraḥ, ʔoren

DESCRIPTION: The laurel is an evergreen tree, native to Palestine, where it grows in the mountains, on Hermon, Tabor, Gilead and Carmel. The oblong leaves are dark green, with a glossy surface, and the flowers are small, white and clustering. The tree may attain a height of 15 m.

Whether or not the laurel is mentioned in the Bible would appear to be a question open to discussion between botanists and linguists. Moldenke maintains that the Hb word ʔezraḥ in Ps 37.35 should be

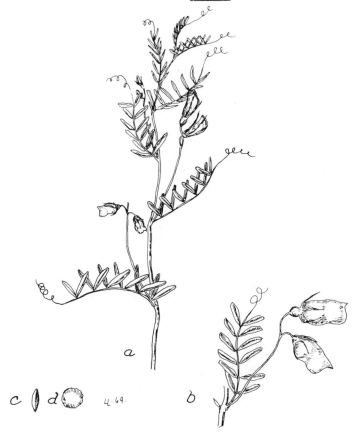

Lentil (*Lens esculenta*)
a. flowering shoot   *b*. pods
c. seed from edge   *d*. seed from side

rendered 'laurel'. The literal translation of the verse is, 'spreading himself like a luxuriant native (tree)' (cf NEB 'rank as a spreading tree in its native soil'). See OTTP, p 100. Most commentators follow a conjecture proposed by the LXX: 'towering like the cedars of Lebanon'.

Most commentaries and dictionaries translate ʔoren in Is 44.14 as 'pine' (as in modern Hb), 'fir tree', or 'ash'. RSV, JB and NEB have 'cedar'. However, ID follows a suggestion by Löw, who for linguistic reasons identifies ʔoren with the laurel.

REFERENCES: ʔezraḥ: Ps 37.35
ʔoren: Is 44.14

Lentil   Lens esculenta

Hebrew: 'adhashah

DESCRIPTION: Among botanists it seems to be beyond question that 'adhashah is the lentil, a small pea-like annual plant with a slender stem, compound leaves bearing five to six pairs of oblong leaflets, and violet flowers. Each of the small pods contains a single seed. Lentils have been cultivated in the Near East from ancient times and they have been an important source of nourishment, as they readily grow even in bad soil. When boiled, lentils turn reddish-brown. In an emergency they may be mixed with cereals for bread-making (Ezk 4.9).

REFERENCES: Gn 25.34; 2 S 17.28; 23.11; Ezk 4.9

Lily   Lilium chalcedonicum, Lilium candidum, Anemone coronaria, Anthemis palæstina, Nymphæa alba, Gladiolus byzantinus

Hebrew: shushan, shoshan, shoshannah

Greek: krinon

DESCRIPTION: It is likely that the Hb word shushan covers more than one species of the lily family, and it may even include other families. Much depends on the context. 1 K 7.26 (2 Ch 4.5) describes the molten brass sea in Solomon's temple, and says that its brim was 'like the brim of a cup, like the flower of a lily'. This comparison between a cup and a flower makes some commentators think not of the lily, but of the Egyptian lotus or water lily (Nymphæa lotus, Nymphæa alba), the shape of which would better serve the purpose of a water basin. Others translate: 'the brim was wrought like the brim of a cup, with flowers of lilies', referring to the ornamentation of the brim. JB translates: 'its rim was shaped like the rim of a cup, like a flower', without saying which flower.

Botanists say that among the many different species of the lily family only one grows in Palestine. Post maintains that this one is Lilium candidum, the white lily or Madonna lily; others say that it is the Lilium chalcedonicum, the red one. The red lily applies better to the quotation in SS 5.13, 'his lips like lilies'. The other half of the verse, 'dropping sweet smelling myrrh', seems, however, to indicate a rare fragrant flower.

Lilies are often mentioned in the Song of Solomon, where it is said that they grow abundantly in valleys and gardens. But the name shushan, 'lily', may be generic, denoting any plant with showy flowers.

In the Psalms the word is mentioned only in the titles, as part of two musical terms whose meaning is unknown to us.

In the NT we find the word krinon, which in Gk literature is often to be understood as Lilium candidum or Lilium chalcedonicum. It is used by Jesus in the Sermon on the Mount, when he says: 'Even Solomon in all his glory was not arrayed like one of these.' Most commentators now think of the Anemone coronaria, the anemone with beautiful bright colours which is to be found on the hills of Galilee, where it would undoubtedly have been seen by the people listening to Jesus.

An interesting theory has been put forward by Ha-Reubeni, a professor of Biblical botany in Jerusalem (quoted by Moldenke). He maintains that Jesus' words indicate that he was not mentioning an especially beautiful or conspicuous flower like a lily or an anemone,

4.69.

Lily (*Anemone coronaria*)

but on the contrary a small and insignificant one, the beauty of which could only be noticed by close study. This has led him to the assumption that the flower in question is Anthemis palæstina, the camomile, a white daisy-like plant. Dalman favours Gladiolus byzantinus, because its purple colour would match Solomon's robe.

REFERENCES: shushan, shoshan, shoshannah: 1 K 7.19, 22, 26; 2 Ch 4.5; titles of Ps 45; 60; 69; 80; SS 2.1, 2, 16; 4.5; 5.13; 6.2, 3; 7.2; Ho 14.5
krinon: Mt 6.28; Lk 12.27

Mallow   Atriplex halimus

Hebrew: malluaḥ

DESCRIPTION: The Hb word malluaḥ is derived from a root m-l-ḥ meaning 'salt', and is usually identified with a species of saltwort, Atriplex halimus, which grows abundantly around the shores of the Dead Sea and in the regions east of Sinai, the country often recognized as Uz, the home of Job. NEB translates as 'saltwort'. It is related to spinach, not to the common mallow. A bushy shrub with oval leaves, it grows up to 1 m tall; in the region of the Dead Sea it may even reach 3 m. The buds and young leaves were eaten by the poor.

REFERENCES: Job 30.4, and probably also 24.24

Dillman suggests that siaḥ in Job 30.4 (RSV 'the leaves of bushes') should probably be more specific: e.g. artemisia or wormwood (q.v.).

DIFFICULT PASSAGE: Job 24.24: Literally, 'They wither and fade like all'. kakol ('like all') is difficult to explain. Most translators, therefore, follow the LXX which reads hōsper molochē, Hb kemalluaḥ (cf RSV 'like the mallow').

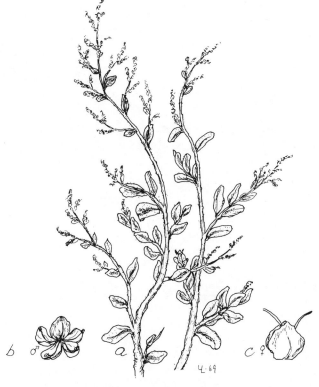

Mallow (*Atriplex halimus*)
a. part of flowering plant
b. flower (male)   *c.* flower (female)

[137]

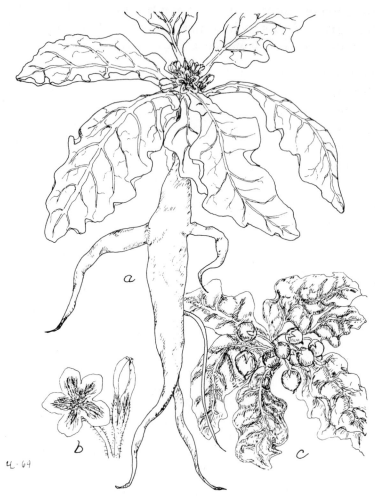

Mandrake (*Mandragora officinarum*)
a. flowering plant with root
b. flower   *c.* plant with fruit

Mandrake, Love Apple   Mandragora officinarum

Hebrew: dudha?im

DESCRIPTION: Commentators agree on the identification of the Hb
dudha?im, which is commonly translated 'mandrakes'. It grows
everywhere in the fields of Palestine and Syria, and on waste
places throughout the Mediterranean area. It is a perennial related to the nightshade, potato and tomato. The stemless herb has

large oval leaves arranged in a rosette, and purple flowers. The yellowish-green fruits, which are rather like plums, ripen during May, 'the days of wheat harvest' (Gn 30.14).

The peculiar shape of the large, fleshy, forked roots, which resemble the lower part of the human body, gave rise to a popular superstition that the mandrake would induce conception. The plant has been used medicinally, its effect being narcotic and purgative. Botanists do not agree concerning its odor, some saying it is fragrant, others calling it fetid. It should be borne in mind that ideas of fragrance differ among people of different cultures. Most commentators translate SS 7.13 'mandrakes' (so RSV).

REFERENCES: Gn 30.14-16; SS 7.13

Manna

Hebrew: <u>man</u>   Greek: <u>manna</u>

DESCRIPTION: The derivation of the Hb word is dubious, so that a precise identification is not available. Some translations connect the word <u>man</u> in Ex 16.15 with the interrogative <u>mah?</u>, 'what?'. Others render the sentence <u>man hu?</u>, 'this is manna'. In Western Aramaic <u>man</u> means 'who'; in Syriac it means 'what'.

Most present-day commentators connect manna with the <u>Tamarix mannifera</u> which grows in the wadis of the Sinai desert. In this they follow an old tradition handed down from Saint Catherine's Monastery at Sinai (founded 530 AD) which says that monks and pilgrims travelling through the desert of Sinai from the third century onward had observed manna falling from tamarisks. It is known that up to our time Bedouin of the Sinai peninsula use the name <u>mann</u> for the honey-like liquid dropping from tamarisks. This is a small tree or bush, 2.7 to 4.5 m tall, with many branches and small scale-like leaves. It grows in the deserts of Palestine and Sinai.

One theory is that manna exudes from the twigs of the tamarisk in heavy drops. This happens in the months of May and June, when the bark of the twigs is punctured by certain small scale-insects

(Coccus manniparus). The manna appears as a sticky, sweet liquid, which quickly hardens and falls to the ground as yellow pellets. Recent investigations, however, indicate that manna is a secretion or excrement from the two scale-lice Najacoccus serpentinus minor and Tradutina mannipara which suck enormous quantities of liquid from the tamarisk twigs in spring in order to collect enough nitrogen for their grubs.

These theories fit the description given by the Bible (Ex 16.20) that the manna had to be collected immediately; what was left soon became 'foul'. But a difficulty is apparent when an assessment is made of the quantity needed for such a numerous people wandering through the desert for forty years. To this must be added the fact that the manna in question is deficient in food value. The analysis indicates glucose, fructose, some pectin, but no protein.

This has caused some commentators to suggest that the Biblical manna was of various kinds. Besides those mentioned above, there is an algal genus Nostoc, which grows up from the moist ground dur-

Melon (*Citrullus vulgaris*)

[140]

ing the night, and a lichen <u>Lecanora esculenta</u>, which grows in the plains and on the mountains of Western Asia. As this is light, it is often carried long distances by the wind. Moreover, it must be remembered that manna was not the only food of the children of Israel. They had dates (Ex 15.27), and they brought cattle with them from Egypt (Ex 12.38). Sometimes they purchased food (Dt 2.6).

REFERENCES: <u>man</u>: Ex 16.15, 31, 35; Nu 11.6, 7, 9; Dt 8.3, 16; Jos 5.12; Ne 9.20; Ps 78.24

<u>manna</u>: Jn 6.31, 49; He 9.4; Rv 2.17

Melon <u>Citrullus vulgaris</u>

Hebrew: ʔabhaṭṭiaḥ

DESCRIPTION: This is a succulent trailing plant which is cultivated in Egypt along the river Nile, where the damp and warm climate makes a single fruit grow to a weight of up to 14 kg. The watermelon is a favourite fruit in Egypt to this day. Beneath the firm greyish-green rind there is an orange-coloured juicy pulp.

REFERENCE: Nu 11.5

Millet <u>Panicum miliaceum</u> (or <u>Sorghum vulgare</u>)

Hebrew: <u>doḥan</u>

DESCRIPTION: Millet, one of the oldest cereals, came originally from India or Persia. It is a grass reaching a height of about 90 cm. The stalks are used as fodder for cattle, while the grain, cooked as a porridge or mixed into bread flour, can be eaten by man. But, like spelt, it is looked upon as an inferior grain compared with wheat, and in Ezk 4.9 it is used to indicate the shortage of cereals caused by a siege.

The name Panicum miliaceum ('thousand-grain') was given to it by the Swedish botanist Linnaeus, because of its fertility.

Post identifies dohan with Sorghum vulgare, the Indian millet, which is a somewhat taller grass than millet.

REFERENCE: Ezk 4.9 (some readings also have it in Is 28.25)

Millet (*Panicum miliaceum*)
a. fruiting head   *b.* flowering spikelet

Mint (*Mentha longifolia*)
a. flowering plant   *b.* flower

Mint   Mentha longifolia

Greek: hēduosmon

DESCRIPTION: Mint is an herb of the mint family, belonging to the labiatæ. The leaves are spear-shaped and notched, and the many-flowered lilac-coloured whorls form conical spikes. It is mentioned only in the NT. The Gk name hēduosmon means 'sweet-smelling', indicating the fragrance of the plant, due to its oils. It grows in ditches, on river banks and even in the mountains. The Jews used mint as a condiment, e.g. when eating milk and cucumber. Mint stems and leaves were scattered over the floors of the synagogues.

[143]

This small, cheap and insignificant plant is mentioned by Jesus in his attack on the Pharisees. According to Dt 12.17; 14.22, 23, the obligation to tithe concerned only grain, wine and oil. Jesus attacks the Pharisees for their meticulous observance of the letter of the law while overlooking the spirit of it, 'judgment, mercy and faith'.

REFERENCES: Mt 23.23; Lk 11.42

Mulberry tree   Morus nigra

Greek: sukaminos

DESCRIPTION: The mulberry tree, a native of Persia but cultivated in Palestine around AD 200, belongs to the genus Morus and to the

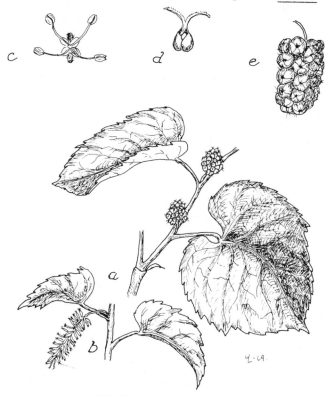

Mulberry (*Morus nigra*)
a. shoot with female inflorescences
b. shoot with male inflorescences
c. male flower   *d.* female flower   *e.* mature fruit

[144]

family Moraceæ. It is a deciduous fruit-tree up to 6 m high with a broad crown. When ripe the berries turn black and contain a sweet red juice.

The black mulberry, moron, is mentioned in 1 Maccabees 6.34 in a peculiar context: the red juice of the berries was shown to the elephants to provoke them to fight.

Apart from this reference, there is no evidence, according to modern botanists and commentators, that the mulberry tree is mentioned in the Bible. The reason for its inclusion in this list is that the AV and other old translations render the Hb word baka? in 2 S 5.23, 24 and 1 Ch 14.14, 15 as 'mulberry trees'. RSV and JB have 'balsam trees' and NEB 'aspens'. Lk 17.6 also mentions the sukaminos which is usually the Gk for 'mulberry tree'. See SYCAMORE.

Mustard   Brassica nigra

Greek: sinapi

DESCRIPTION: The seed described in the parable of Jesus as 'the smallest of all seeds' is considered by most translators to be the common black mustard seed, Brassica nigra.

Brassica nigra is now an annual garden herb, but in former days it grew wild in the fields of Palestine; the Jews sowed it in their fields and not in their gardens (Mt 13.31; Strack-Billerbeck I, 669).

In our day the seeds of mustard, which are contained in linear pods, are not considered to be the smallest of all seeds (a distinction held by the orchid). But in the days of Jesus the smallest quantity of something was proverbially compared with 'a mustard seed' (Mt 17.20). The black mustard seed has a section of 1 mm and weighs 1 mg. The seed was used as a condiment and for preserving food. It contains an oil and was used medicinally.

The mustard plant does not usually grow as tall as a tree, but travellers relate that they have passed through mustard fields in which all the plants exceeded the height of a man, and where birds were actually sheltering in the 'branches'. The stem of the mustard plant may be as thick as a man's arm. The description of it as a 'tree' in the parable is, therefore, not misleading.

Some commentators have suggested that the seed mentioned in the parable was not that of the black mustard, but of a different plant, <u>Salvadora persica</u>. But this is found in the valleys of the Jordan river, not in the fields. Moreover, its seeds are too large to fit the description given in the Gospels.

REFERENCES: Mt 13.31; 17.20; Mk 4.31; Lk 13.19; 17.6

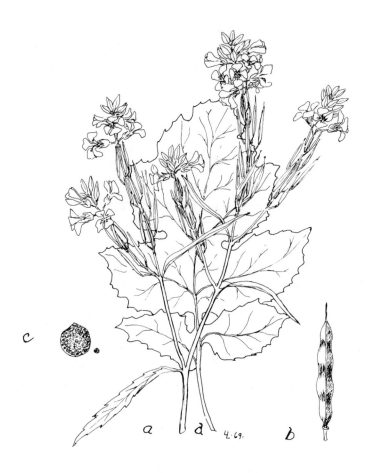

Mustard (*Brassica nigra*)
a. flowering shoot *b.* pod
c. seed *d.* lower leaf

Myrrh (*Commiphora myrrha*)
a. branch with fruit
Stacte (*Commiphora opobalsamum*)
b. fruit   *c.* female flower   *d.* male flower

Myrrh   Commiphora myrrha (Cistus salvifolius)

Hebrew: mor (loṭ)   Greek: smurna

DESCRIPTION: Myrrh is a dark-red gum with a strong aroma and a
bitter taste. It exudes from a bush or tree belonging to a family of
the burseraceæ which grows in Arabia, Abyssinia and on the Somali
coast of East Africa. It is not native to Palestine. This tree or bush
has a great number of knotted branches. The gum exudes from the
branch as a thick light-coloured paste which, when exposed to the
atmosphere, soon hardens and takes on a brownish colour. The
finest myrrh was the resin secreted of itself (rather than by artifi-
cial incision) through the bark, mor-deror, mentioned in Ex 30 as an
ingredient of the holy ointment, and most likely also in SS 5.5, mor
obher, 'liquid myrrh'.

[147]

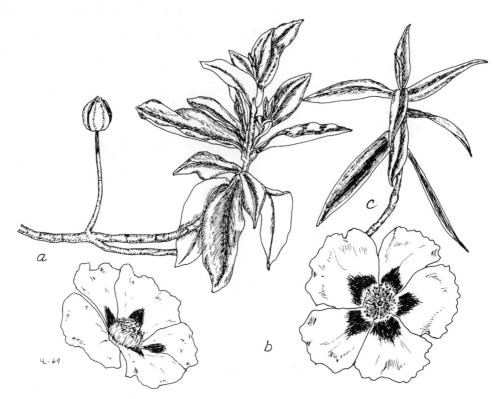

Myrrh (*Cistus ladaniferus*)
a. shoot with fruiting capsule and leaf
b. flowers *c.* narrow leaf

Some rich and distinguished people might have had 'a mountain of myrrh' in their garden. But the tree was not native to Palestine and the import of myrrh made it an expensive luxury. This should be borne in mind when reading Es 2.12, Ps 45.8, Pr 7.7, SS 1.13 and Mt 2.11, where the magi brought royal gifts for the new-born baby.

Myrrh was also used for embalming the dead, Jn 19.39. Nicodemus must have been a rich man since he could afford such a quantity of myrrh and aloes.

See also BALM, STACTE and SPICES.

REFERENCES: <u>mor (lot)</u>: Ex 30.23; Es 2.12; Ps 45.8; Pr 7.7; SS
               1.13; 3.6; 4.6,14; 5.1,5,13
          <u>smurna</u>: Mt 2.11; Mk 15.23; Jn 19.39

DIFFICULT PASSAGES: Mk 15.23 uses esmurnismenos, the perfect passive participle of smurnizō, which means 'treated or flavoured with myrrh'. It was the Jewish custom to offer a strong aromatic drink of wine to a man sentenced to death. The idea was to relieve his pain. Jesus did not accept this, because he wished to be fully conscious until the last moment.

In Gn 37.25; 43.11 lot is rendered 'myrrh' in RSV and NEB (JB 'resin'). The Hb word is identified by some scholars with ladanum (not to be confused with laudanum), an aromatic gum exuded from the leaves of the cistus-rose, Cistus salvifolius, which is native to Palestine. An argument in favour of ladanum is the fact that Gn 43.11 mentions gifts from the country to a foreign land. Cf Ex 30.34 where sheheleth, 'onycha', refers to a species of the genus Cistus (but see ONYCHA). The 'galbanum' of Ex 30.34, helbenah, is similarly an aromatic resin extracted from various species of the genus Ferula, akin to fennel or dill.

Myrtle   Myrtus communis

Hebrew: hadhaṣ

DESCRIPTION: The myrtle is a native of Asia Minor and the Mediterranean countries, where it grows mostly in valleys on moist soil. It is an evergreen tree or bush, which may reach a height of 1.5 m. The dark glossy leaves are dense on the branches, and the flowers are white or pink. The whole plant gives off an agreeable odour. It was used by the Jews in the Feast of Tabernacles (Ne 8.15).

REFERENCES: Ne 8.15; Is 41.19; 55.13; Zech 1.8,10,11

DIFFICULT PASSAGES: Zech 1.8,10,11: Some commentators follow the LXX and read 'mountains', harim, instead of the Masoretic text 'myrtles', hadhassim.

'ets-'abhoth, Lv 23.40; Ne 8.15; Ezk 6.13; 20.28, which literally means 'leafy or branchy trees', or 'trees having interwoven foliage', is sometimes identified with the myrtle. RSV has 'leafy tree'.

Narcissus   Narcissus tazetta

Hebrew: ḥabhatstseleth

DESCRIPTION: There is little evidence to support the traditional rendering 'rose', and it is likely that the flower referred to is the narcissus. This grows with several flowers on one stem, and in Palestine is a bright golden yellow.

Walker (following Moldenke) suggests that the 'rose of Sharon' (SS 2.1) may be a red tulip, Tulipa sharonensis.

Myrtle (*Myrtus communis*)
a. part of flowering plant   *b*. fruit

[150]

In Song of Solomon RSV and JB have 'rose'; in Isaiah RSV 'crocus', JB 'jonquil'. NEB has 'asphodel', a kind of lily.

REFERENCES: SS 2.1; Is 35.1

Nard, Spikenard   Nardostachys jatamansi

Hebrew: nerd   Greek: nardos

DESCRIPTION: Nard grows in the Himalayan countries of Bhutan and Nepal, and in Kashmir. It belongs to the Valerian family. The root and lower part of the stems are fragrant. When dried, they are used

Nard (*Nardostachys jatamansi*)

in perfume, and the ointment, known in ancient times, is appreciated
even now by the women of India. In ancient times perfumed ointment
and oil were kept in sealed jars, which could be opened only by break-
ing the neck. The fact that perfume made from the nard plant had to
be imported (by the Phoenicians) from India made the ointment mentioned in the NT 'very costly'.

This precious perfume becomes a symbol of wealth and beauty,
as in SS 4.13,14. This passage does not indicate that nard grew in
Palestine; the whole description in these verses gives a picture of
an ideal flower-garden, like Paradise.

REFERENCES: nerd: SS 1.12; 4.13,14
nardos: Mk 14.3; Jn 12.3

DIFFICULT PASSAGES: Mk 14.3; Jn 12.3: nardos pistikē is generally
translated 'pure' or 'genuine nard'. The word pistikos in the NT occurs only in these two passages, and its derivation is doubtful. AG
(p 668) suggest that the word may be derived from Sanskrit picita,
the name of the plant Nardostachys jatamansi.

Nettle   Urtica dioica, Urtica pilulifera

Hebrew: harul

DESCRIPTION: The context suggests any kind of desert shrub. BDB
identifies it with the chick pea, Cicer arietinum. RSV translates
'nettle', though 'thorn-bushes' might well be better. JB has 'nettle'
or 'thistle', NEB 'scrub' or 'weeds'.

In addition to the above-mentioned, two other species of the
genus Urtica have been found in Palestine, Urtica caudata and Urtica
urens. It is an annual plant with broad, notched leaves. Stem and
leaves are covered with stinging hairs, and the flowers are small
and green. It grows in unweeded gardens and in areas where cultivation is neglected.

REFERENCES: Job 30.7; Pr 24.31; Zeph 2.9

Nettle (*urtica dioica*)
upper part of flowering plant

Nutmeg flower (Black Cummin) Nigella sativa

Hebrew: qetsaḥ

DESCRIPTION: This is an annual plant of the Crowfoot family, 30 to 50 cm high. The flowers have yellowish or blue petals and many stamens; the leaves are feathery and finely divided. The fruit is a capsule and contains many small black aromatic seeds, which like pepper are used for seasoning.

AV translates the Hb word 'fitches', RSV and NEB 'dill', JB

'fennel'. But the description given by Isaiah of the way of threshing the fruits undoubtedly refers to <u>Nigella</u>. See DILL.

REFERENCES: Is 28.25, 27

Nutmeg flower (*Nigella sativa*)
a. plant   *b.* fruit with seeds (cut through)
c. two sepals with petals transformed to nectaries
d. one petal transformed to nectary   *e.* drop of nectar

Oak tree   Quercus coccifera,   Quercus ægilops

Hebrew: <u>ʔelon</u>, <u>ʔallon</u>

DESCRIPTION: Like the Hb <u>ʔelah</u> or <u>ʔallah</u> (RSV 'terebinth'), the word <u>ʔelon</u> or <u>ʔallon</u> is often simply rendered 'big tree'. There is no doubt, however, that the Hb authors sometimes distinguish between the two names, as for instance in Is 6.13 and Ho 4.13 (see RSV).

[154]

The Hb words may refer to different species of oak, but there is no unanimity among modern botanists as to which of the six species found in Palestine are referred to in the Biblical quotations. Only two of them will be described.

Post identifies ʔallon with Quercus coccifera, an evergreen which grows in the mountains and has short-stemmed, firm and oval spiny-toothed leaves and solitary or twin acorns. A deciduous species is Quercus ægilops, which reaches a height of 15 m and with its heavy trunk may well symbolize the beauty and strength often spoken of in the OT. The leaves are leathery with stalks, glossy on the surface, oblong and serrated. The acorns are very large.

See also TEREBINTH. NEB translates ʔelon as 'terebinth', ʔallon as 'oak'.

REFERENCES: ʔelon: Gn 12.6; 13.18; 14.13; 18.1; Dt 11.30; Jos 19.33; Jg 4.11; 9.6, 37; 1 S 10.3
ʔallon: Gn 35.8; Is 2.13; 6.13; 44.14; Ezk 27.6; Ho 4.13; Am 2.9; Zech 11.2

Oak (*Quercus coccifera*)

Olive tree, Oil tree   Olea europaea, Elaeagnus angustifolia

Hebrew: zayith, 'ets shemen

Greek: elaia, agrielaios (wild olive tree)

DESCRIPTION: The olive tree is characteristic of the Palestinian flora and is mentioned very often in the Bible. It is a native of Asia Minor and Syria, from where it spread over North Africa and the Mediterranean countries of Europe. According to Dt 8.8, the olive tree was growing in the land of Canaan before the Israelites conquered it.

The trunk of an olive tree is very broad and rough, and is often twisted. The crown of the tree consists of four to six heavy branches, each with several clusters of twigs, and the whole tree may reach a height of 24 m. The leaf is oblong and evergreen, and it has become famous in world literature because of the role it played in the history of the Flood (Gn 8). Since then the olive leaf and the dove have become symbols of peace.

The olive tree grows very slowly and may attain a great age. It is difficult to eradicate an old olive, because it will always sprout from the root. An old root surrounded with fresh young shoots is an illustration to the psalmists of a crowd of children in a Jewish home (Ps 128.3).

The flowers, which appear in May, are bell-shaped and yellowish, with a sweet odour. The fruit, shaped like a prune but smaller, is green until September when it ripens and becomes black. Thirty-one percent of the ripe fruit is oil. Not until the tree is thirty years old can the full yield be expected, but at that age it is very fruitful (Ps 52.8; Je 11.16; Ho 14.6). The fruit on the upper branches which cannot be reached from the ground are beaten or knocked down with sticks (Is 17.6; 24.13).

Grafting is also mentioned. St. Paul's reference to grafting in Ro 11.17, 24 is intentionally strange. The usual course of action was to graft cultivated branches onto wild trees. Paul, however, speaks in opposite terms, comparing the Gentiles to the wild shoots which are

Olive tree (*Olea europæa*)
a. flowering shoot *b*. flower
c. section of fruit *d*. shoot with fruit

grafted on to the cultivated olive tree, the people of Israel, so as to share in its blessing.

The wild olive tree (Olea europæa oleaster), which is a native of Palestine, is regarded (probably wrongly) by some as the ancestor of the domestic olive tree.

REFERENCES: zayith: Consult a concordance
'ets shemen: ('fat tree', 'tree of oil', 'oil tree')
1 K 6.23, 31, 32, 33; Ne 8.15; Is 41.19
elaia (olive tree, fruit of olive): Mt 21.1; 24.3;
26.30; Mk 11.1; 13.3; 14.26; Lk 19.37; 22.39;
Jn 8.1; Ro 11.17, 24; Jas 3.12; Rv 11.4
elaion (olive grove): Lk 19.29; 21.37; Ac 1.12

DIFFICULT PASSAGE: 1 K 6, describing the building of the temple, mentions a kind of wood which is rendered by some translators 'olive wood', by others 'wild olive wood'. It is probably advisable to follow Moldenke and others who maintain that the olive wood is of

[157]

no use as a building material or for carving because the trunk of the tree is rather short and usually contorted. They therefore suggest <u>Elæagnus angustifolia</u>, the narrow-leaved oleaster, a small tree of the Oleaster family 4.5 to 6 m tall, whose small leaves are blue on the surface and silvery underneath. The fruits, almost the size of an olive, yield an oil which is unfit for food but often used for medicinal purposes. It grows in Palestine and the wood is hard and suitable for carving. It is sometimes called 'wild olive', but it is not a member of the olive family.

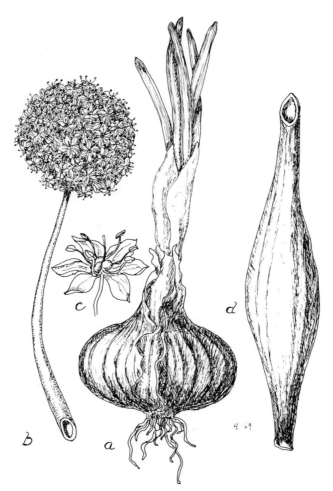

Onion (*Allium cepa*)
a. bulb   *b.* inflorescence
c. flower   *d.* lower part of stem

Onion Allium cepa   **Garlic** Allium sativum   **Leek** Allium porrum

Hebrew: betsel (onion) shum (garlic) ḥatsir (leek)

DESCRIPTION: There does not seem to have been any discussion about the translation of the three Hb words in Nu 11.5, for they were already rendered 'onion', 'garlic' and 'leek' in the early translations into Greek (LXX), Latin (Vulgate) and Syriac (Peshitta).

The Egyptian onion (Allium cepa) belongs to the lily family. It is a perennial vegetable, the bulb growing much larger than onions do in Western Europe. The pink or white flowers are situated in globu-

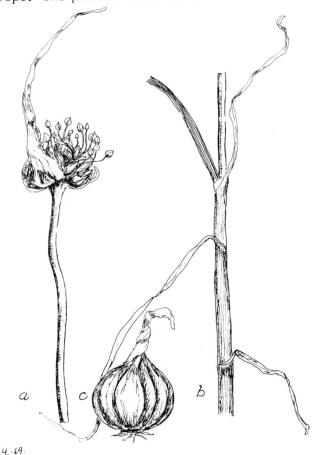

4.69.

Leek (*Allium sativum*)
a. & b. stem with inflorescence and bulbils
c. bulb

lar umbels. The onion is probably a native of Persia or Egypt. It was cultivated from early days, and constituted an important item of diet, as it is sweet-tasting, nourishing and easy to digest, besides being cheap.

The garlic (Allium sativum) is also a member of the lily family, in appearance very much like the onion. Since ancient times it has been cultivated in Egypt and Palestine, where it is a favourite dish, and is both eaten raw and cooked. Its characteristic strong flavour appealed to the Jews and Egyptians, but it was disliked by the Romans and ancient Greeks.

The leek (Allium porrum) differs in appearance from the garlic and onion, in that the bulb is oblong. This vegetable also has been a very popular food among the Egyptians from very early days.

REFERENCE: Nu 11.5

DIFFICULT PASSAGE: The Hb ḥatsir is only to be translated 'leek' in this passage. In all other passages it must be translated 'grass' or 'herb'. See GRASS.

Palm   Phoenix dactylifera

Hebrew: tamar, timorah, tomer

Greek: phoinix

DESCRIPTION: A characteristic feature of the palm is its straight trunk, unusually tough, which has no branches but ends in a circle of great leaves; it may reach a height of 18 to 24 m. The root is strong and fibrous.

Seen at a distance, the shape of the palm tree is very attractive, and it was often used as an ornament by architects (cf 1 K 6.29; Ezk 40.16 and 41.18).

In Hebrew the leaf of the palm tree is called kippah, a word derived from the Hb 'hand'. A palm leaf may have some similarity to a human hand with spread fingers. We may, however, find more resemblance between a palm leaf and a feather. In the Bible palm leaves are often inaccurately called 'palm branches'; cf Jn 12.13 in the Greek and in several translations, e. g. RSV. The leaves may grow up to 2.7 m long. In the beginning they grow upward, but are bent down by their own weight.

There can be no doubt that the palm mentioned in the Bible is the date palm, Phoenix dactylifera, which is quite common in Palestine and Egypt. This tree may live up to two hundred years, and it is only fully developed after thirty years. Palm trees seem to grow

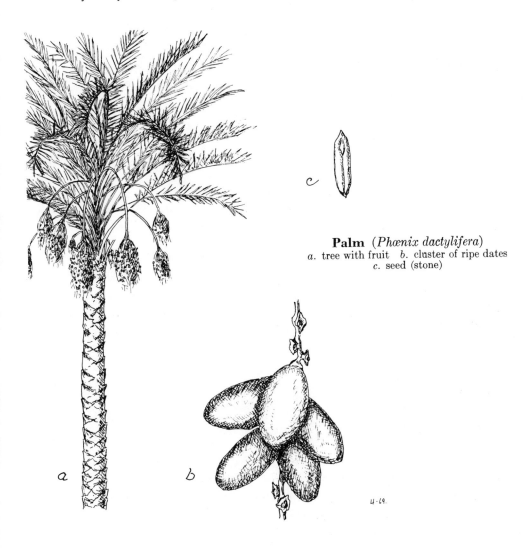

Palm (*Phœnix dactylifera*)
a. tree with fruit   *b.* cluster of ripe dates
c. seed (stone)

particularly well in the area around Jericho, for the Bible calls it 'the city of palm trees' (Dt 34.3). Josephus confirms this in his Jewish Wars (IV.8.3).

Certain women in the OT were named after this tree (Gn 38.6; 2 S 13.1; 14.27).

REFERENCES: tamar, timorah: Consult a concordance
tomer: Jg 4.5; Je 10.5 (in the latter passage, 'post' or 'scarecrow')
phoinix: Jn 12.13; Rv 7.9

DIFFICULT PASSAGES: Some commentators (Budde) and dictionaries (Gesenius) maintain that dates are also mentioned in the Bible, namely in SS 7.7-8 (implied in RSV, explicitly in JB and NEB). The word in question is the Hb ʔeshkol, the meaning of which is 'cluster' It usually stands for clusters of grapes, but in SS 1.14 it signifies 'cluster of henna blossoms', and the context in SS 7.7-8 argues for 'cluster of dates'.

ʔel is a Hb word which signifies any large tree, and is usually translated 'terebinth' or 'oak'. Gesenius also gives the translation 'palm tree' in Is 1.29; 57.5; 61.3; Ezk 31.14.

nahal is generally translated 'valley' or 'creek'. Gesenius mentions the possibility of translating this word 'palm' in the following passages: Nu 24.6; Job 29.18; SS 6.11. This translation for Job 29.18 follows a conjecture suggested by the Vulgate (sicut palma), to read kenahal 'like the palm' instead of kahol 'like the sand'. See also OTTP, p 82f.

Pine, Aleppo Pine Pinus halepensis

Hebrew: berosh, beroth

DESCRIPTION: The identification of the Hb berosh is far from certain and many different suggestions about the identity of the evergreens and conifers mentioned in the Bible have been made by botanists and commentators. Some follow KB and translate 'Phoenician juniper' (JB has 'juniper' in some places). This, however, does

Aleppo Pine (*Pinus halepensis*)

not fit Ps 104.17 which presumes a high tree in which the stork is building its nest. Post suggests the cedar, others the cypress. RSV and JB usually translate 'cypress', NEB 'pine'.

The Aleppo pine is the largest and noblest among the pines growing in the Lebanon. It is a conifer, native to the Mediterranean area, which grows 3 to 18 m tall with diffuse ascending branches and yellowish twigs. The bark of the younger trees is smooth and grey. The leaves or needles are arranged in bundles of two or three, and the cones are reddish-brown. The timber is suitable for beams in buildings.

[163]

REFERENCES: <u>berosh</u>: 2 S 6.5; 1 K 5.8,10; 6.15,34; 2 K 19.23;
2 Ch 2.8; Ps 104.17; Is 14.8; 37.24; 55.13;
60.13; Ezk 27.5; 31.8; Ho 14.8; Na 2.3; Zech
11.2
<u>beroth</u>: SS 1.17

DIFFICULT PASSAGES: 2 S 6.5: The Masoretic text reads: <u>bekhol</u>
<u>'atse bheroshim</u> 'with all articles (or, instruments) of fir (or cy-
press) wood'. It may be better to follow the reading of 1 Ch 13.8:
<u>tekhol 'oz ubheshirim</u> 'with all their might and with songs'.

For Na 2.3 see OTTP, p 246.

Pine, Brutian Pine <u>Pinus brutia</u>

Hebrew: <u>tidhhar</u>

DESCRIPTION: The Brutian pine grows in the mountains of northern
Palestine, where Post found it in Gilead and Lebanon. It reaches a

Pistachio nuts (*Pistacia vera*)
a. part of flowering branch, showing leaves folded and unfolded
b. female flower   *c.* male flower   *d.* seed from edge
e. seed from side

height of 3 to 10 m. Its branches are whorled, the leaves twin and rather thick; longer, darker and more rigid than those of the Aleppo pine. The cones are arranged in whorls, 3 to 6 at a time. Moldenke identifies tidhhar with this conifer.

BDB and some other interpreters (e.g. Buhl) follow the Vulgate in translating 'elm', which would fit the circumstance that the Syriac name for this tree, Ulmus campestris, is dadar. But Moldenke does not believe that it is indigenous to Palestine. The leaves of the common elm tree are oblong, serrated and hairy or smooth. The yellow or green flowers are arranged in clusters and the fruit is winged.

Other translators, including RSV and JB, render 'plane tree' (q.v.). NEB has 'fir'.

REFERENCES: Is 41.19; 60.13

Pistachio nuts   Pistacia vera,   Pistacia Palæstina

Hebrew: botnim

DESCRIPTION: RSV, JB and NEB are correct in rendering botnim as 'pistachio nuts'. The pistachio is a native of Asia Minor, but is found also in Palestine and Syria, especially in the region of Damascus and Beirut. But it is not a product of Egypt, and so it is suitable for a gift to that country (Gn 43.11). It is the fruit of a small tree which has a broad crown. The fruits of the Pistacia Palæstina are smaller than those of Pistacia vera and are less tasty. The fruit ripens in October, and is almost the same size as a hazel-nut, longish and triangular. It has a red shell and a green and oily kernel. It has a pleasant flavour, and is eaten raw or roasted with pepper and salt. It is also used for seasoning chocolates.

REFERENCE: Gn 43.11

DIFFICULT PASSAGES: It is doubtful if the name of a location in the tribe of Gad, betonim (Jos 13.26), has any connection with botnim.

The nut mentioned in SS 6.11 is undoubtedly the walnut, Juglans regia.

[165]

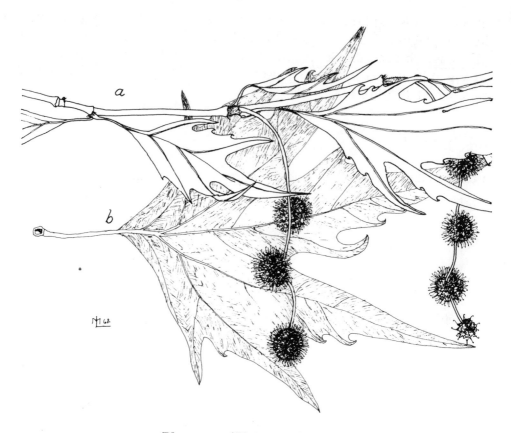

Plane tree (*Platanus orientalis*)
a. leafy shoot with fruiting heads   *b.* leaf

Plane tree   Platanus orientalis

Hebrew: 'armon

DESCRIPTION: The oriental plane tree is a native of Palestine and
Mesopotamia, where it grows near water. The large leaves, in
shape much like those of the vine, are dark green on the surface
and woolly underneath. The long branches spread in every direc-
tion and offer a comfortable shade. The flowers are green and inconspicuous, and the fruits are like small globes covered with
spikes. The plane tree may reach a considerable height and a
great age.

The Hb word may be derived from a root: 'bare' or 'naked',
referring to a peculiarity of the tree's bark, which scales off in

sheets. This explains why Jacob chose branches from a plane for his 'stratagem'. The Vulgate in both passages identifies the Hb with platanus; so does the Septuagint in Gn 30. AV has 'chestnut tree'. RSV and JB also translate tidhhar as 'plane' in Is 41.19; 60.13. For this see PINE (BRUTIAN PINE).

REFERENCES: Gn 30.37; Ezk 31.8

Poison, Gall, Hemlock   Conium maculatum

Hebrew: ro?sh, rosh

DESCRIPTION: The two Hb words indicate poison or venom of serpents (e.g. Dt 32.33; Job 20.16); but in some passages (e.g. Ho 10.4)

Poison (*Conium maculatum*)
a. part of flower with inflorescence
b. fruiting head   *c*. seed   *d*. part of stem

[167]

it may be understood as a poisonous plant, Conium maculatum, the hemlock, which is quite common all over Palestine. It is a perennial or biennial, erect and many-branched with leaves like those of the carrot. The tiny white flowers are arranged in umbels, and the root is white and tapering. All parts of the plant --root, leaves, and the small fruits -- contain a dangerously poisonous oil.

REFERENCES: Dt 29.18; 32.32, 33; Job 20.16; Ps 69.21;
Je 8.14; 9.15; 23.15; La 3.5,19; Ho 10.4; Am 6.12

Pomegranate   Punica granatum

Hebrew: rimmon

DESCRIPTION: The pomegranate is native to many countries in North Africa and Western Asia. The Hb word rimmon may stand for

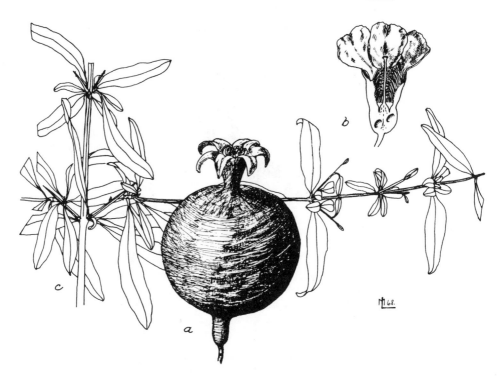

Pomegranate (*Punica granatum*)
a. fruit   *b.* section of flower   *c.* branch

the pomegranate tree, the fruit, or the artistic ornaments in the shape of pomegranates such as were to be found in the temple of Solomon (1 K 7.18), or on the skirts of Aaron's ephod (Ex 28.33).

The pomegranate tree is 3.6 to 4.5 m high with dark-green, spear-shaped leaves, and branches carrying thorns. It has scarlet, yellow and white flowers, and a fruit (actually a berry) about the size of an orange, with a hard red or yellow rind. The pulp is divided into 9 or 10 partitions which hold the numerous seeds. The pulp is delicious and very refreshing to eat because of its copious juice. The seeds yield a syrup called grenadine. The flowers are used in the treatment of dysentery.

Poplar (*Populus euphratica*)
a. twig with male inflorescence
b. twig with female inflorescence
c. mature fruit capsule and one seed
d. & e. different leaf shapes

This picturesque and beautiful tree and its fruit were very popular with artists: see the description of Solomon's temple and the garments of the priests.

The name of a locality, Rimmon, e. g. Jos 15.32, probably indicates the presence of many pomegranates some time in the past.

The Syrian god Rimmon mentioned in 2 K 5.18 is hardly to be connected with the pomegranate.

REFERENCES: Consult a concordance

Poplar (Euphrates Poplar) Populus euphratica

Hebrew: 'erebh

DESCRIPTION: The Euphrates poplar is a high tree and very common on the banks of brooks and rivers in the Orient. It has two forms of leaves, some broad and oval and others (on the younger shoots) spear-shaped and oblong like the leaves of the willow. Walker identifies the tree with the willow, Salix alba, which may be true of Lv 23.40 because in Palestine the poplar is confined to the Jordan valley. JB and RSV both alternate between 'willow' and 'poplar'. But the translation 'poplar' is justified in all passages by the fact that the Arabic name of this tree, gharab, is cognate with the Hb word. The flowers of the poplar are catkins, the fruits are capsules with hairy seeds. See also STORAX.

REFERENCES: Lv 23.40; Job 40.22; Ps 137.2; Is 15.7; 44.4

Purslane Suaeda asphaltica

Hebrew: ḥallamuth

DESCRIPTION: The meaning of this word is uncertain, but it is usually taken to mean 'purslane' (as in RV mg and RSV). This is a succulent plant of the Judean desert, related to Atriplex halimus (see MALLOW). It is very dependent upon rain, and scarcely appears at all in dry periods. It grows to a height of 45 cm and has tubular leaves and greenish flowers.

However, as Hb peasants would use the same name for different plants and different names for the same plant with no feeling of contradiction, the words for 'mallow' and 'purslane' may well both refer to Atriplex halimus.

AV, RV and JB have 'the white of an egg', and NEB 'mallow'.

REFERENCE: Job 6.6

Reed and Rod Arundo donax, Typha angustata, Cyperus papyrus, Scirpus

Hebrew: qaneh, suph, gome?, ?aghmon, ?ebheh

Greek: kalamos, kalamē

DESCRIPTION: The different kinds of grasses will not always be easy to identify by means of the Hb or Gk names, and many translations may have to depend on a conjecture.

Arundo donax is a giant reed, much taller than a man, which grows in rivers and waters like the Nile, and is well known in Palestine and Syria; in the Jordan valley it grows in almost impenetrable thickets. The stem can easily be broken (2 K 18.21), and is used for many purposes, e.g. as a measuring rod (Ezk 40.3, 5; 42.16-19), but it is also flexible and shaken by the wind (Mt 11.7). The flowers are white and grow in plumes.

suph: ID identifies it with cattail, Typha angustata. It often occurs in connection with yam, 'sea': yam-suph, 'sea of rushes', the Red Sea, e.g. Ex 10.9, and consult a concordance.

gome? is usually regarded as papyrus, Cyperus papyrus (e.g. RSV of Job 8.11; Is 18.2). ?aghmon, 'rush', 'bulrush', is identified by ID with the genus Scirpus, a lake plant lower than the reed, with flexible stems. ?ebheh is probably Arundo or papyrus.

REFERENCES: qaneh: Consult a concordance
             suph: Ex 2.3, 5; Is 19.6; Jon 2.5 (RSV 'weeds')
             gome?: Ex 2.3; Job 8.11; Is 18.2; 35.7
             ?aghmon: Job 41.2 (RSV 'rope'),20; Is 9.14; 58.5

[171]

ʔebheh: Job 9.26

<u>kalamos</u>: Mt 11.7; 12.20; 27.29, 30, 48; Mk 15.19, 36;
  Lk 7.24; 3 Jn 13; Rv 11.1; 21.15, 16

<u>kalamē</u>: 1 Co 3.12, 'stalk' or 'straw'. According to
  AG, the meaning 'stubble' (RSV) is possible but
  less likely.

DIFFICULT PASSAGES: qaneh in Is 19.6 and 35.7 is identified by
Moldenke with <u>Cyperus papyrus</u>.

  In Gn 41.5, 22, according to Gesenius qaneh means 'stalk of
grain'. In 1 K 14.15; 2 K 18.21; Job 40.21; Ps 68.30; Is 19.6; 35.7; 36.6;

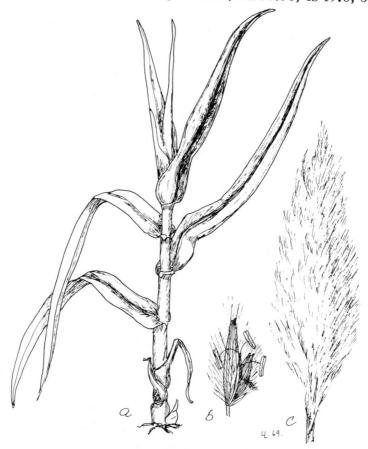

Reed (*Arundo donax*)
a. young plant *b.* flowering spikelet
c. fruiting head with mature seeds

42.3 and Ezk 29.6 translate 'waterplant' or 'reed'. In some cases it is used figuratively to mean weak support.

Ex 30.23; SS 4.14; Je 6.20; 43.24; Ezk 27.19 are to be understood as an aromatic reed, a constituent of anointing oil, imported from a far country, perhaps Andropogon calamus aromaticus. (Moldenke identifies Is 43.24 with Saccharum officinarum.) Ezk 40.3, 5; 42.16-19 'measuring rod'. Ezk 40.5-8; 41.8 is a 'unit of measure' (six cubits). Is 46.6 '(beam of) scales'. Ex 25.31, 32, 35; 37.17, 18, 'shaft or branch of lamp-stand'. In Job 31.22 it is used figuratively of the shoulder-joint (shekhem).

Rue (*Ruta graveolens*)
a. part of plant   *b.* flower   *c.* fruit

[173]

?aghmon in Job 41.2 = rush twisted and used as cord. For the same word in Job 41.20 see OTTP, p 92. ?aghammim in Je 51.32 is ?aghmon according to BDB. Burning of swamp plants is common practice among inhabitants of such areas in order to accelerate their growth. (RSV 'the bulwarks are burned with fire'.) Volz reads, instead of sarepu 'are burned', sharebu 'the swamps are drained'.

3 Jn 13 'pen'.

Rue Ruta graveolens, or Ruta chalepensis

Greek: pēganon

DESCRIPTION: Rue is a plant or shrub, which in Mediterranean countries grows from 90 cm to 1.5 m tall and has yellowish flowers and strong-smelling leaves.

Both species grow wild in Palestine and Syria and were probably also cultivated there in NT times. Rue was used as a condiment, and its fresh leaves were used to heal certain diseases, insect stings and snake bites.

On tithing see CUMMIN.

REFERENCE: Lk 11.42

Saffron Crocus sativus (or Carthamus tinctorius)

Hebrew: karkom

DESCRIPTION: Among the various fragrant plants mentioned in the description of a costly garden in SS 4 we find the Hb karkom. This is generally considered to be the blue-flowered saffron crocus, Crocus sativus, whose long thread-like stigmas, when dried and pulverized, yield a yellow dye used in ancient times for colouring food, clothing and walls. Mixed with oil this aromatic product also served as a condiment, a perfume and a medicine.

Whether the Crocus sativus was grown in Palestine in Biblical times cannot be stated definitely. It does not grow there today. SS 4 mentions karkom among several foreign spices.

[174]

It has been suggested that karkom may be an entirely different plant, Carthamus tinctorius. This native of the Middle East is a member of the thistle family, growing 90 cm to 1.2 m tall, with red florets which yield a dye used for colouring clothing and food.

REFERENCE: SS 4.14

Spelt   Triticum spelta,   Triticum dicoccum

Hebrew: kuṣṣemeth (kuṣṣemim)

DESCRIPTION: Spelt is a member of the grass family allied to wheat. It has loose ears, and its triangular grains do not loosen from the chaff when ripening.   It has been known from ancient times in Egypt,

Saffron (*Crocus sativus*)
a. flowering plant   *b.* stigma

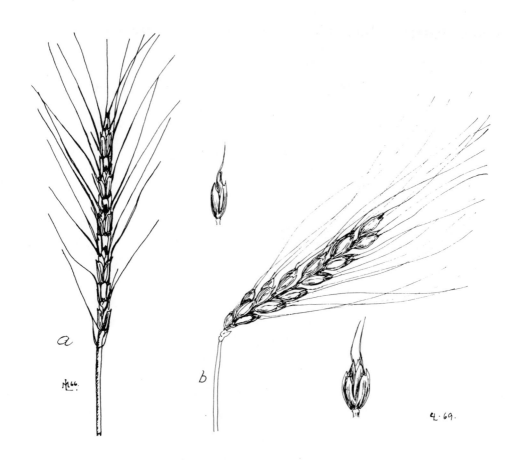

Spelt
a. *Triticum spelta*
b. *Triticum dicoccum*
spike and spikelets

where it is found in the tombs. While inferior to wheat, it will grow in less fertile and humid soil.

Post identifies the Hb word with Triticum spelta, and ID with wild emmer, Triticum dicoccum.

REFERENCES: Ex 9.32; Is 28.25; Ezk 4.9

[176]

Spices, Balsam, Balsam tree   Commiphora opobalsamum

Hebrew: <u>b</u>osem, <u>b</u>esem, <u>b</u>asam

DESCRIPTION: 'Spices' is the word used by most modern translations to render these Hb words. Southern Arabia (Sheba) was one of
the places from which they were imported (2 Ch 9.1). They were
used in the anointing oil (Ex 30.23). In SS 5.13; 6.2 they are probably
to be identified with 'balm of Gilead' (see NEB 'balsam' in 6.2).. But
the Hb words refer to various spices which are not always identifi-
able.

ID is inclined to identify them with <u>Commiphora opobalsamum</u>,
the 'balm of Gilead': a shrub or small tree which is not a native of
Gilead but of Southern Arabia. It grows to. 4.5 m and has stiff
branches, trifoliate leaves and white flowers. The branches exude
a pleasant-smelling resin, which soon hardens when exposed to the
air. The gum is used for perfume and for medicinal purposes. In
Biblical times it was cultivated in the Jordan valley near Jericho,
perhaps also in Gilead.

Balsam (*Astragalus tragacantha*)
a. shoot *b.* flower *c.* pod

[177]

Walker says that besem was Astragalus tragacantha, a very small plant 60 cm high, which grows everywhere in Palestine. The resin exudes from the thorns and is collected during the day by rubbing the plant with a ball of cotton.

See also BALM, MYRRH and STACTE.

REFERENCES: Consult a concordance

Stacte Commiphora opobalsamum

Hebrew: nataph, lot

DESCRIPTION: Stacte is a resinous, aromatic gum exuding from some species of Commiphora opobalsamum. Other suggestions include Styrax officinalis or Cistus salvifolius, but this is rejected by ID, which adds that it is doubtful whether the cistus rose is gum-bearing.

Stacte is a spice which was used for incense. See also BALM, MYRRH and SPICES. (For illustration of stacte, see page 147.)

REFERENCES: nataph: Ex 30.34 (JB 'storax'; NEB 'gum resin')
lot: Gn 37.25; 43.11 (RSV and NEB 'myrrh'; JB 'resin')

Storax tree Styrax officinalis

Hebrew: libhneh

DESCRIPTION: The Hb name, which may perhaps be derived from labhan, 'white', has often been identified with the white poplar, Populus alba (by Moldenke, many commentators, RSV, JB and NEB). We follow Post, ID and others, who take it as Styrax officinalis. JB translates nataph as 'storax'. See STACTE.

This is a small tree or shrub 3 to 6 m high, a native of Asia Minor, Syria and Galilee. Its white flowers resemble those of the orange tree. Its oval leaves are green above and white and cottony below.

Storax (*Styrax officinalis*)
a. flowering shoot *b.* fruit

In Ho 4.13 three different sacred trees are mentioned, under the shadow of which idolatrous incense-burning took place. LXX understands the white poplar to be meant here, whereas it has the storax in Gn 30. But there is no reason for making a distinction between the two references.

REFERENCES: Gn 30.37; Ho 4.13

Sycamore   Ficus sycomorus

Hebrew: shiqmah   Greek: sukomorea

DESCRIPTION: The sycamore tree belongs to the Nettle family, like the mulberry and fig trees. It grows in many places in Palestine, especially in the plain, from Gaza to Jaffa and Haifa, and in the Jericho valley.

It is a broad heavy tree, 7.50 to 15 m high. The branches are strong and large, growing out from the trunk very low down so that the tree is easy to climb. It stands firmly on the ground as the roots are very long. Its wood was used for buildings, and the fact that the Egyptians used it for their mummy coffins is evidence of its durability.

[179]

The leaves are evergreen and heart-shaped, and the fruit looks like figs, but its taste is unpleasant. However, it was eaten by poor people, and Amos (7.14) was a gatherer of sycamore fruit. The Hb verb may indicate the way the sycamore fruits were eaten, so that the proper translation may not be 'gatherer of sycamore fruit', or 'cultivator', but 'one who nips (with a nail or with iron) the fruits to make them edible'.

Sycamore (*Ficus sycomorus*)
a. part of young stem with leaf-bearing twig
b. dwarf shoots with fruit

Sycamore wood, though used in building, was poorly thought of in comparison with cedar (Is 9.10).

In the NT the tree is mentioned in the story of Zacchaeus (Lk 19.4) who climbed it in order to see Jesus.

REFERENCES: shiqmah: 1 K 10.27; 1 Ch 27.28; 2 Ch 1.15; 9.27; Ps 78.47; Is 9.10; Am 7.14

sukomorea: Lk 19.4

Tamarisk (*Tamarix aphylla*)
a. flowering shoot   *b.* tip of branch
c. flower   *d.* fruit

DIFFICULT PASSAGE: NEB is probably right in translating Lk 17.6: 'you could say to this sycamore-tree, Be rooted up and replanted in the sea', even though the Gk is sukaminos, which is generally translated 'mulberry tree'. Löw suggests that Luke did not differentiate between the sycamore and the mulberry. The height and weight of the sycamore make it a more adequate illustration of what is said here about the force of faith. This is also supported by the fact that LXX translates shiqmah as sukaminos. But most modern translations have 'mulberry tree' (q.v.).

Tamarisk   Tamarix aphylla, T. gallica

Hebrew: ?eshel

DESCRIPTION: The tamarisk is a small, fast-growing tree with durable wood, to be found abundantly in deserts, dunes and salt marshes.

Tamarix aphylla is leafless and has green branches and a wide crown. It has small white flowers, and its fruit is a capsule with feathery seeds.

NEB translates Gn 21.33 as 'Abraham planted a strip of ground'.

REFERENCES: Gn 21.33; 1 S 22.6; 31.13

Terebinth   Turpentine tree, Pistacia terebinthus

Hebrew: ?elah, ?allah

DESCRIPTION: ID maintains that the 'nuts' mentioned in Gn 43.11 are the fruits of Pistacia terebinthus palæstina (see PISTACHIO NUTS). Post and Moldenke, however, identify them with the Pistacia vera, and they render the Hb ?elah as 'terebinth', of which the above-mentioned P. T. palæstina is a variety.

The terebinth may reach a height of 7.5 to 9 m, and its broad crown, heavy branches and thick trunk give it an impressive appearance like that of the oak tree. The tree, which usually stands alone, affords pleasant shade. It is native to the Mediterranean countries. It is not an evergreen, and its flowers are small and inconspicuous. The stem contains aromatic turpentine, a resinous juice, which flows out when the bark is cut.

Most dictionaries simply translate ?elah as 'big tree', as with ?elon (see OAK). It is practically impossible to distinguish between these two.

REFERENCES: Consult a concordance.

Terebinth (*Pistacia terebinthus*)
a. branch with fruit *b.* female flower *c.* male flower

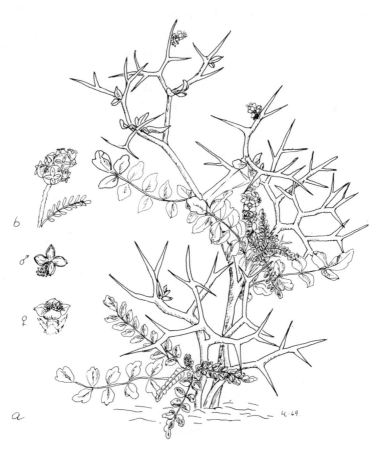

Thorn (*Poterium spinosum*)
a. young flowering plant   *b.* fruit

Thorn, Thistle, Brier, Bramble
Lycium europaeum, Poterium spinosum, Solanum incanum (he-dheq), Centaurea, Scolymus

Hebrew: ṣeneh, ʾaṭadh, barqanim, ḥoaḥ, dardar, ḥedheq, naʿatsuts, ṣirpadh, ṣir, ṣillon, qots, qimmosh, shamir, shayith, tsen, sekh, mesukkah

Greek: akantha (thorns), akanthinos (made of thorns), tribolos (thistle), batos (thorn bush)

DESCRIPTION: A dry country like Palestine produces a rich variety of thorns and thistles, and it is not always possible to determine which particular plants are referred to. They are characteristic of an area which is uncultivated or neglected. 'Thorns and thistles' may thus be a symbol of the punishment and judgment of the Lord (Gn 3.18; Is 7.23-25), or of the work of false prophets (Mt 7.16). It is true that many thorn bushes bear beautiful flowers, but one can never gather grapes or figs from them. The thorn bush is, however, suitable for hedges.

Bible readers and commentators have naturally always been eager to identify the plant from which the crown of thorns was plaited by the soldiers. Zizyphus has been suggested from the time of Linnaeus, who added the name 'spina Christi' to it. The difficulty, however, is that this does not grow in the region where the event took place. Modern botanists sometimes suggest Poterium spinosum, which forms a mass of vegetation all over the country. It grows leaves twice a year, and has small red flowers. The thorns are numerous and cover the bush completely.

MacKay writes (p 170), "Old Roman coins show some of the Emperors wearing spiked crowns, so the thorns may have been chosen to resemble a royal diadem, and not to cause pain. Laurel leaves made up the traditional chaplet of the conqueror, and a thorny plant resembling laurel may have been used."

Moldenke quotes Smith's suggestion that the burning bush (Ex 3.2) may have been the crimson-flowered mistletoe Loranthus acaciæ, which is quite common in Palestine where it grows on thorny shrubs and trees.

REFERENCES: seneh: Ex 3.2, 3, 4; Dt 33.16
ʔaṭadh: Gn 50.10, 11; Jg 9.14, 15; Ps 58.9
barqanim: Jg 8.7, 16
ḥoaḥ: 1 S 13.6; 2 K 14.9; 2 Ch 25.18; 33.11; Job 31.40; 41.2; Pr 26.9; SS 2.2; Is 34.13; Ho 9.6
dardar: Gn 3.18; Ho 10.8
ḥedheq: Pr 15.19; Mi 7.4
na'atsuts: Is 7.19; 55.13
ṣirpadh: Is 55.13
ṣir: Ec 7.6; Is 34.13; Ho 2.6; Am 4.2; Na 1.10
ṣillon: Ezk 2.6; 28.24

[185]

qots: Gn 3.18; Ex 22.6; Jg 8.7,16; 2 S 23.6; Ps 118.12;
        Is 32.13; 33.12; Je 4.3; 12.13; Ezk 28.24; Ho 10.8
qimmosh: Pr 24.31; Is 34.13; Ho 9.6
shamir: Is 5.6; 7.23-25; 9.18; 10.17; 27.4; 32.13; Je
        17.1; Ezk 3.9; Zech 7.12
shayith: Is 5.6; 7.23-25; 9.18; 10.17; 27.4
tsen: Job 5.5; Pr 22.5
sekh: Nu 33.55
mesukkah, mesukah, mesukah: Pr 15.19; Is 5.5;
        Mi 7.4
akantha: Mt 7.16; 13.7,22; 27.29; Mk 4.7,18·
        Lk 6.44; 8.7,14; Jn 19.2; He 6.8
akanthinos: Mk 15.17; Jn 19.5
tribolos: Mt 7.16; He 6.8
batos: Mk 12.26; Lk 6.44; 20.37; Ac 7.30,35

DIFFICULT PASSAGES: In Jg 8.7,16 barqanim is translated by some
commentators as 'threshing sledges' rather than 'briers'.

    seneh is identified by Löw as Rubus sanctus, by Post as Cassia
obovata. ?atadh is Lycium europaeum.

    In 1 S 13.6 hoah is thickets as hiding places. Some read holim,
'holes' (so RSV). hoah in Job 41.2 and 2 Ch 33.11 should be rendered
'hook' or 'ring'. sir in Am 4.2 is also to be rendered 'hook' or
'ring'.

    In Ezk 2.6 instead of sallonim, the plural of sillon, some read
solim which means 'resisting'.

    shamir in Je 17.1; Ezk 3.9; Zech 7.12 is not to be translated
'thorn' but 'adamant'.

    tsen in Job 5.5 may perhaps be deleted (as suggested by Cheyne)
as a doublet of tsammim.

    2 Co 12.7 has the well-known passage about the 'thorn in the
flesh'. The Gk word (skolops) literally means 'a pointed stake'.

Tumbleweed Whirling Dust, A Rolling Thing   <u>Gundelia tournefortii</u>

Hebrew: <u>galgal</u>

DESCRIPTION: The commentators disagree on the identification of
<u>galgal.</u> Literally the word means 'a wheel'. NEB has 'thistledown';
RSV translates 'whirling dust', but see margin for 'tumbleweed'.
Botanists have discovered at least thirty species of tumbleweeds in
Palestine. When ripening, these plants curve in and form a globe
which breaks off just above the ground and is carried along the
ground by the wind like a rolling ball or 'whirling dust'. This is
true, for instance, of <u>Gundelia tournefortii.</u> The dried calyx of this
thistle is wheel-shaped, and when it is blown along by the wind it
may cause horses to shy.

Moldenke and several others suggest the 'rose of Jericho',
<u>Anastatica hierochuntica,</u> but this plant is very rare in Palestine,
and also it sticks to the ground for years and never rolls over the
surface, according to ID. This states the most common tumbleweeds

Tumbleweed (*Anastatica hierochuntica*)
a. part of plant with leaves and flowers
b. plant knotted around ripe seeds

[187]

in Palestine to be: Gundelia tournefortii, Cachrys goniocarpa, Aellenia autrani, and Salsola kali.

REFERENCES: Ps 83.13; Is 17.13

Vine (vineyard, vinegar, wine, grape)   vitis vinifera

Hebrew: gephen, zemorah, sarigh, soreqah
           kerem: vineyard
           yayin, ḥemer, mashqeh, ṣobheʔ, shekhar, shemer, tirosh,
              mezeg, soreq: wine
           ʔeshkol hagephen, ʔeshkol 'anabim, 'enabh: grape

Greek: ampelos
          ampelōn: vineyard
          oinos: wine   gleukos: sweet, new wine
          sikera (from Aram. sikera = Hb shekar): a strong drink different from wine
          botrus: cluster of grapes   staphulē: bunch of grapes

DESCRIPTION: The grapevine has been known from ancient times and it was common among the Canaanites. Its home is said to be the hills of Armenia and around the Caspian Sea, and a reference to this may be found in the story of Noah (Gn 9) who planted a vineyard on his return from mount Ararat (in Armenia), where the ark rested. Wine is seldom mentioned in the patriarchal stories. Abraham did not offer wine to his guests (Gn 18), but he accepted it from Melchizedek (Gn 14). At that time the use of wine was characteristic of the Canaanites in contrast to the strict and simple moral life of the nomads. But the distinctions disappeared after the Israelites had settled in the country. The Nazirites and the Rechabites abstained from wine for religious reasons. But Jotham's fable (Jg 9) and the parables of Jesus prove that wine was a common drink among the Jews.

A vineyard was often put 'on a very fertile hill' (Is 5), not only a hill with fertile ground, but also a place which could be reached by the sun from all sides. But there were vineyards also in the valleys, e.g. the valley of Sharon, and even in the dry South (Negeb), to

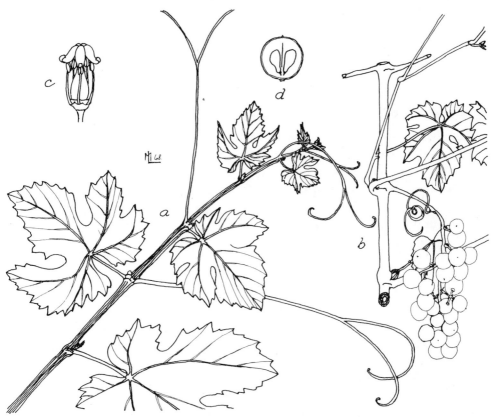

Vine (*Vitis vinifera*)
a. tip of shoot   *b.* part of stem with cluster of grapes
c. flower   *d.* section of grape

which the geographical names bear witness (Nu 13.23).   A vineyard demands work.   After the ground has been prepared, a fence must be erected and a watch tower built. If all the preparatory work has been carefully done, the owner is justified in expecting a good harvest, and his disappointment if this does not happen is understandable (Is 5).

The Bible also mentions vines that grow like trees and which may develop a trunk of quite considerable diameter. A man may 'sit under his vine' (Mi 4.4); or vines may creep along the ground ('a low spreading vine', Ezk 17.6), or be supported by forks, or climb over trees. Some translations illustrate this, e. g. JB: 'It covered the mountains with its shade, the cedars of God with its branches' (Ps 80.10).

[189]

The best-loved vines were those planted near dwellings. The phrase which is often repeated in the historical books: 'Every man under his vine and under his fig tree' has become almost proverbial for the peaceful conditions which the Israelites enjoyed during the reign of Solomon.

What kinds of grapes were raised in those days cannot, of course, be known. It is impossible to draw any conclusions from present-day conditions. Since the middle ages Palestinian wine has been made from white grapes, but much seems to indicate that in Biblical times the large red grapes were grown. Red grape juice is mentioned, 'the blood of grapes' (Gn 49.11; Dt 32.14; Pr 23.31; Is 63.2). To these OT texts might be added the words of Jesus at the Last Supper, when he compares blood and wine (Mt 26.27), and Rv 14.20. Further, the word soreq is derived from a root which means 'bright red'.

The wine mentioned in the Bible was fermented and contained alcohol. There is nothing to indicate that they knew how to keep grape juice unfermented by methods like modern pasteurization. Without special treatment it would not have been possible to keep the juice unfermented more than one or two days in that climate. Also, the Bible has many warnings against intoxication.

REFERENCES: gephen: Consult a concordance
zemorah: Nu 13.23; Is 17.10; Ezk 15.2 (and 8.17); Na 2.2
sarigh: Gn 40.10,12; Joel 1.7
soreqah: Gn 49.11
kerem: Consult a concordance
yayin: Consult a concordance
ḥemer: Dt 32.14; Is 27.2
mashqeh: means any kind of drink, a butler or a drinking vessel: Gn 40.2,5,9,13,20,21,23; 41.9; Lv 11.34; 1 K 10.5,21; 2 Ch 9.4,20; Ne 1.11; Is 32.6
ṣobhe?: Is 1.22; Ho 4.18; Na 1.10
shekhar: Lv 10.9; Nu 6.3; 28.7; Dt 29.6; Jg 13.4,7,14; 1 S 1.15; Ps 69.12; Pr 20.1; 31.6; Is 5.11,22; 24.9; 28.7; 29.9; 56.12; Mi 2.11

shemer: Ps 75.8; Is 25.6; Je 48.11; Zeph 1.12

tirosh: Gn 27.28, 37; Nu 18.12; Dt 7.13; 11.14; 14.23;
    18.4; 28.51; 33.28; Jg 9.13; 2 K 18.32; 2 Ch 31.5;
    32.28; Ne 5.11; 10.37, 39; 13.5, 12; Ps 4.7; Pr 3.10;
    Is 24.7; 36.17; 62.8; Je 31.12; Ho 4.11; 7.14; 9.2;
    Joel 1.10; 2.24; Mi 6.15; Hg 1.11; Zech 9.17

mezeg: SS 7.2

soreq: Is 5.2; Je 2.21

ʔeshkol: Gn 40.10; Nu 13.23, 24; Dt 32.32; SS 1.14;
    7.7, 8; Is 65.8; Mi 7.1

'enabh: Gn 40.10, 11; 49.11; Lv 25.5; Nu 6.3; 13.20, 23;
    Dt 23.24; 32.14, 32; Ne 13.15; Is 5.2, 4; Je 8.13; Ho
    3.1; 9.10; Am 9.13

oinos: Mt 9.17; 27.34; Mk 2.22; 15.23; Lk 1.15; 5.37,
    38; 7.33; 10.34; Jn 2.3, 9, 10; 4.46; Ro 14.21; Eph
    5.18; 1 Ti 3.8; 5.23; Rv 6.6; 14.8, 10; 16.19; 17.2;
    18.3, 13; 19.15

gleukos: Ac 2.13

sikera: Lk 1.15

botrus: Rv 14.18

staphulē: Mt 7.16; Lk 6.44; Rv 14.18

DIFFICULT PASSAGES: Nu 13.23. zemorah: Travellers in Palestine have often expressed their wonder at the size and weight of the grape clusters. Nevertheless, the description of the cluster in Nu 13.23 has caused some commentators to think of another fruit, e. g. the banana. But if bananas had grown in this area, they would undoubtedly have been mentioned elsewhere in the Bible.

Ezk 8.17. The translation of zemorah: In all other quoted passages the word is translated 'a branch or twig of the vine'. Here the meaning is dubious. The written text is often translated: 'They are stretching (literally, sending) out the branch to their nose.' This is to be understood as the ritual of some idolatrous worship. The verb shalah would, however, not be adequate in this connection, meaning as it does 'to send out'. Nor does this gesture, a mere detail in an idolatrous Persian ritual, fit God's extreme anger (v 18). Some modern translators, therefore, adopt the reading of the qere (scribal correction) 'my nose' (i. e. God's nose) instead of 'their nose', and

[191]

render the word zemorah 'bad odour' or 'male organ', indicating an obscene gesture.

Some translators render yayin in Gn 9.24; 1 S 1.14; 25.37 as 'drunkenness'.

ṣobheʔ: Ho 4.18 = drunkenness or winebibbers (see BDB).

Na 1.10: literally the words mean 'and like their drunkard drunken', i.e. drunk according to their nature, or, altogether intoxicated with wine. Some translators maintain that the text is corrupt and that these words should be omitted as a dittography (see OTTP, p 246). Others (e.g. Elliger) instead of sebhuʔim read lebhiʔim (lions), referring to the foregoing 'thorns' in which the wild animals hide (Je 4.7).

For Mt 27.34 and Mk 15.23 see MYRRH.

The symbolism of the vine is apparent from such passages as Gn 49.22 and Ezk 19.10: a strong and active man or woman, whose life has been fruitful, can be compared with the vine.

Vinegar   In some places (Ru 2.14; Ps 69.21; Pr 10.26; Mk 15.36 and parallels) the Bible mentions a sour drink, Hb ḥomets, Gk oxos, which is sometimes translated 'vinegar'. It is supposed that this drink was made by making the grape juice ferment artificially, for instance by adding barley. It may also be that a germ of the aceto-bacter family was known in those days. Mixed with water it was a popular drink among soldiers and workmen (Latin posca), as it was cheaper than wine, and good for quenching thirst. Without water it would be very strong and intoxicating, and could even cause unconsciousness.

Walnut Juglans regia

Hebrew: ʔeghoz

DESCRIPTION: The 'garden of nuts' (AV) or 'nut orchard' (RSV) is now generally considered to be a garden of walnut trees.

The walnut tree is native to Persia and Western Asia. It is very probable that it was grown in the orchards of the rich in Biblical times. Josephus records the widespread cultivation of walnut trees in Palestine in his day.

It is a handsome tree with a broad crown and fresh green oval leaves which offer welcome shade and an agreeable fragrance. The fruits are nuts, covered by a thick rind which yields a brown dye.

REFERENCE: SS 6.11

Walnut (*Juglans regia*)
a. twig with young fruit   b. twig with male and female flowers   c. fruit cut through   d. walnut

Weeds Lolium (temulentum)

Greek: zizanion

DESCRIPTION: Lolium temulentum is an annual plant, 50 to 100 cm high with an erect stem bearing five to seven leaves. Before it bears fruit Lolium is almost indistinguishable from wheat, among which it often grows as a weed. Only when the two come into ear can they be distinguished.

Weed (*Lolium temulentum*)
a. & *b.* Lolium temulentum
c. & *d.* barley (Hordeum vulgare)

It is hardly possible to weed a wheatfield and get it free from Lolium, as the roots of both grasses will be entangled. Thus the householder in the parable says (Mt 13.29): "No, lest in gathering the weeds you root up the wheat along with them."

Lolium seed retains its germination capacity for several years, so that in rainy seasons the weed may suddenly appear in such quantities that the poor farmer believes that his wheat has changed into weeds. Heavy rainfall furthers the growth of Lolium but slows down that of wheat. The farmer might let the two grow together until harvest, when the weed was separated and bound in bundles; or he might use a strainer after the threshing, because the grain of the weed is smaller than that of the wheat. It was necessary to be on guard against Lolium, because it is poisonous.

AV and RV translate as 'tares'; JB and NEB as 'darnel'.

REFERENCES: Mt 13.25, 26, 27, 29, 30, 36, 38, 40

DIFFICULT PASSAGE: KB quotes Dalman who suggests that bo'shah in Job 31.40 ('foul weeds') be understood as Lolium temulentum. (Note the misprint in KB, p 106: Solium temulentum should be Lolium te-mulentum. Lisowsky repeats KB's mistake.)

Wheat Triticum æstivum and Triticum compositum

Hebrew: ḥiṭṭah   Greek: sitos, aleuron, semidalis

DESCRIPTION: Wheat is one of the oldest cultivated plants in the world. It has been found in prehistoric sites by the Swiss lakes and in Egyptian tombs, and is known to have been cultivated in Mesopotamia and Palestine.

Among the several different kinds of wheat, at least two are mentioned in the Bible, Triticum æstivum and Tr. compositum; the former is the commonly known present-day kind, and the latter is the Egyptian 'mummy' wheat with seven ears, the one mentioned in Pharoah's dream (Gn 41.5). Wheat is usually mentioned first among the resources of a country (Dt 8.8; Ezk 4.9). After nomadic life had

[195]

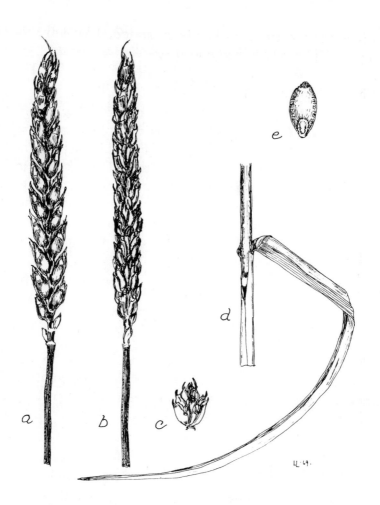

Wheat (*Triticum œstivum*)
a. & b. spike from different angles   *c.* spikelet
d. part of stem with leaf   *e.* seed

ended with Saul and David, agriculture developed and wheat became an export (1 K 5.11).

In Palestine wheat is sown in December, some weeks after barley, and wheat harvest is a week or two later than barley harvest. The time, April at earliest, depends on the temperature and climate of the region.

In the parable of the sower Jesus speaks of seed which fell on good soil having a yield up to a hundredfold. This is no exaggeration although it is not the rule. It has been stated, however, that one seed can yield up to a hundred and fifty grains.

REFERENCES: ḥiṭṭah: Consult a concordance
sitos: Mt 3.12; 13.25, 29, 30; Mk 4.28; Lk 3.17; 12.18; 16.7; 22.31; Jn 12.24; Acts 27.38; 1 Co 15.37; Rv 6.6; 18.13. The diminutive sition is found in Ac 7.12 (some scholars read sita instead of sitia).
aleuron 'meal' (made of wheat): Mt 13.33; Lk 13.21
semidalis 'fine flour', the finest grade of wheat flour: Rv 18.13

DIFFICULT PASSAGES: It should be noted that in Mk 4.28 and Lk 12.18 sitos is rendered 'grain' (in general) by most translators.

Wormwood (*Artemisia arborescens*)

Wormwood   Artemisia judaica

Hebrew: la'anah   Greek: apsinthos, cholē

DESCRIPTION: A plant of the genus artemisia, which may grow to
the size of a bush. There are several species and varieties. Artemisia judaica is native to Palestine; its main stem has side shoots covered with small woolly green leaves. The juice of the leaves has a
bitter taste and may, if drunk unmixed, be noxious, but mixed in the
right proportions it can be a useful medicine. In some passages
wormwood symbolizes God's punishment, or suffering and sorrow.

REFERENCES: la'anah: Dt 29.18; Pr 5.4; Je 9.15; 23.15; La 3.15,19;
             Amos 5.7; 6.12
             apsinthos: Rv 8.11
             cholē: Mt 27.34 cf Ac 8.23

DIFFICULT PASSAGES: LXX translates la'anah 'gall' (Gk cholē) in
La 3.15 and Pr 5.4; but also uses the word 'gall' to translate ro'sh
in Dt 29.18, Ps 69.21 (ro'sh is an unidentified poisonous plant, see
POISON). It therefore may be justifiable to translate cholē in Mt
27.34 'wormwood'.

Bibliography

Arndt, William F., and Gingrich, F. Wilbur. A Greek-English Lexicon of the New Testament and Other Early Christian Literature. Chicago: Univ. of Chicago Press, 1957.

Avigad, Berlinger and Silberstein. Carmel Flowers. Haifa: Department of Education, 1964.

Bare, Garland. Plants and Animals of the Bible. London: United Bible Societies, 1969.

Bentzen, Agge. Handbog i Kristendomskundkab. Copenhagen: Munksgaard, 1942.

Benzinger, Immanuel. Hebräische Archäologie. Leipzig: Eduard Pfeiffer, 1927.

----------. "Kings" in Kurzer Hand-Kommentar zum Alten Testament. Freiburg: J. C. B. Mohr, 1899.

Bertholet, A. "Leviticus" in Kurzer Hand-Kommentar zum Alten Testament. Tübingen: J. C. B. Mohr, 1901.

Bodenheimer, F. S. Animal and Man in Bible Lands. Leiden: E. J. Brill, 1960.

Bratcher, Robert G., and Nida, Eugene A. A Translator's Handbook on the Gospel of Mark. Leiden: E. J. Brill, 1961.

Brown, Francis; Driver, S. R., and Briggs, Charles A. A Hebrew and English Lexicon of the Old Testament. Oxford: Clarendon Press, 1959.

Budde, Karl. "Samuel" and "Song of Solomon" in Kurzer Hand-Kommentar zum Alten Testament. Tübingen: J. C. B. Mohr, 1902 and 1898.

Buhl, F. P. W. Jesaja. Copenhagen: Gyldendalske Boghandel, 1912.

van Buren, E. D. The Fauna of Ancient Mesopotamia as Represented in Art. Vol. 18 of Analecta Orientalia. Rome: 1938.

Cheyne, T. K. "Isaiah" in The Polychrome Bible. Leipzig: J. C. Hinrichs, 1899.

Dalman, G. H. Arbeit und Sitte in Palästina. Gütersloh: C. Bertelsmann, 1928-1964.

Davis, John D., and Gehman, H. S. Westminster Dictionary of the Bible. Philadelphia: Westminster Press, 1944.

Driver, S. R. "Leviticus" in The Polychrome Bible. Leipzig: J. C. Hinrichs, 1898.

Duhm, Bernhard. "Job" in Kurzer Hand-Kommentar zum Alten Testament. Tübingen: J. C. B. Mohr, 1897.

Epstein, Wilhelm. Die Medizin im Alten Testament. Stuttgart: F. Enke, 1901.

Edgecombe, Winnie S. Some Major Weeds of the North Beka'a. Beirut: American University, 1959.

Elliger, K. "Job" in Das Alte Testament Deutsch. Göttingen: 1951.

Feilberg, C. G. La Tente Noire. Copenhagen: Nationalmusæets Skrifter, 1944.

Feveile, Johannes. Jødeland paa Jesu tid. Copenhagen: P. Haase og Son, 1948.

Fohrer, Georg. Vol. XVI of Kommentar zum Alten Testament. Güterslohe: Verlagshaus, 1963.

----------. "Ezekiel" in Handbuch zum Alten Testament. Tübingen: J. C. B. Mohr, 1955.

Galling, Kurt. Biblisches Reallexikon. Tübingen: J. C. B. Mohr, 1937.

Gesenius, Wilhelm. Hebräisches und Arämaisches Wörterbuch zum Alten Testament. Berlin: Springer Verlag, 1954.

Hastings, James. Dictionary of the Bible. Revised. Edinburgh: T. & T. Clark, 1963.

Hauck, D. F. "Luke" in Theologischer Handkommentar zum Neuen Testament. Leipzig: 1934.

Hehn, Victor. Kulturpflanzen und Hausthiere. Berlin: Gebrüder Borntraeger, 1894.

Herner, Sven. Die Natur im Alten Testament. Lund: 1940.

Hertzberg, H. W. Samuel I & II, a Commentary. London: S.C.M. Press, 1964.

Hjerl-Hansen, B. Kapernaum. Copenhagen: 1940.

The Interpreter's Dictionary of the Bible, 4 vols. New York: Abingdon Press, 1962.

Kautzsch, E. (ed.). Die Heilige Schrift des Alten Testaments. Tübingen: J. C. B. Mohr, 1922.

King, Eleanor. Plants of the Holy Scriptures. New York: N. Y. Botanical Garden, 1948.

Kinzler, A. Biblische Naturgeschichte. 1902.

Koehler, Ludwig, and Baumgartner, Walter. Lexicon in Veteris Testamenti Libros. Leiden: E. J. Brill, 1958.

Lewysohn, Ludwig. Zoologie des Talmuds. Frankfurt-am-Main: J. Baer, 1858.

Lisowsky, Gerhard. Konkordanz zum Hebräischen Alten Testament. Stuttgart: Württembergische Bibelanstalt, 1958.

Löw, I. Die Flora der Juden, I - IV. Vienna: Verlagder Kohut Foundation, 1934.

MacKay, Alastair I. Farming and Gardening in the Bible. Emmaus, Pa.: Rodale Press, 1950.

Meissner, Bruno. Babylonien und Assyrien. Heidelberg: C. Winter, 1920-1925.

Moldenke, H. N. and A. L. Plants of the Bible. New York: Ronald Press Co., 1952.

Moortgat, Anton. Vorderasiatische rollsiegel. Berlin: Gebr. Mann, 1940.

Noth, Martin. The Old Testament World. London: Black, 1966.

----------. Exodus, a Commentary. London: S.C.M. Press, 1962.

----------. Leviticus, a Commentary. London: S.C.M. Press, 1965.

----------. Numbers, a Commentary. London: S.C.M. Press, 1968.

Olsen, H., and Madsen, H. Investigation on Pseudo-Rumination in Rabbits. 1940.

Parmelee, A. All the Birds of the Bible. London: Lutterworth Press, 1960.

Paterson, A. Palace of Sennacherib. The Hague: 1915.

Pederson, J. Israel, Its Life and Culture, vols. I - IV. Oxford: The University Press, 1947.

Peterson, W. W. Das Tier im Alten Testament. 1928.

Post, G. E. Flora of Syria, Palestine and Sinai. Beirut: American Press, 1932.

Procksch, Otto. "Genesis" in Kommentar zum Alten Testament. Leipzig: A. Deichert, 1924.

Reicke, Bo; and Rost, Leonard. Biblisch-Historisches Handwörterbuch. Göttingen: Vanderhoeck & Ruprecht, 1962.

Riehm, E. K. A. Handwörterbuch des biblischen Altertums. Bielefeld und Leipzig: Velhagen & Klasing, 1893.

Robinson, T. H. "Jonah" in Handbuch zum Alten Testament. Tübingen, J. C. B. Mohr, 1964.

Rudolph, W. "Ruth," "Song of Solomon," and "Lamentations" in Kommentar zum Alten Testament. Gütersloh: Gerd Mohn, 1962.

Schmoller, Alfred. Handkonkordanz zum griechischen Neuen Testament. Stuttgart: Württembergische Bibelandstalt, 1958.

Schneller, L. Kender du Landet. Copenhagen: Schonbergske Forlag, 1923.

Smith, J. Bible Plants. 1878.

Stave, Erik. Israel i helg och söcken, I - II. Uppsala: Lendblad, 1919.

Strack, Hermann L., and Billerbeck, Paul. Kommentar zum N. T. aus Talmud und Midrasch. Munich: Beck, 1922.

Tristram, H. B. The Fauna and Flora of Palestine. London: The Committee of the Palestine Exploration Fund, 1884.

Volz, Paul. "Jeremiah" in Kommentar zum Alten Testament. Leipzig: A. Deichert, 1928.

Walker, W. All the Plants of the Bible. London: Lutterworth Press, 1958.

Ward, J. Seal Cylinders of Western Asia. London: 1910.

Weiser, Artur. "Job" in Das Alte Testament Deutsch. Göttingen: Vandenhoeck & Ruprecht, 1956.

Wellhausen, Julius. "Psalms" in The Polychrome Bible. Leipzig: J. C. Henrichs, 1904.

Woolley, D. L. Ur Excavations, I - III. London: British Museum, 1936-1964.

Zahn, Theodor. Das Evangelium des Mätthaus. Leipzig: A. Deichert, 1910.

Index of English and Latin Terms

Morus nigra 144
mosquito 30, 35-36
moth 55-56
mountain sheep 38, 75, 76
mouse 57
mulberry tree 144-145, 182
mule 57-58
Muridae 57
Musca vicina 30
muskmelon 113
mustard 145-146
myrrh 104, 105, 135, 147, 149, 178
myrtle 149, 150
Myrtus communis 149, 150

Najacoccus serpentinus 140
Naja haje 72
narcissus 150-151
Narcissus tazetta 150
nard 151-152
Nardostachys jatamansi 151, 152
nettle 152, 153
Nigella sativa 117, 153, 154
night hag 59, 62
night hawk 59, 60, 61
night jar 59, 62
night owl 61
Nostoc 140
nutmeg 153-154
nuts 165, 192, 193
Nymphaea alba 134, 135;
    N. lotus 135

oak 20, 128, 154-155, 162
Oedipoda migratoria 53
oil tree 156-158
Olea europaea 156, 157
oleaster 158
olive tree 156-158
onion 24, 158, 159-160
onycha 60, 149
Origanum maru 129, 130
Ornithogalum umbellatum 24
orris 105
Orthoptera 53
oryx 3, 47
Oryx leucoryx 2, 3
osprey 83, 84
ossifrage 84

ostrich 59, 60, 61
otis 66
Otus scops 4, 65
Ovis laticaudata 75;
    O. tragelaphus 76
owl 4, 15, 16, 18, 19, 24, 51-52, 59, 60, 61, 62, 65, 71
ox 6, 62-63

palm 160-162
Palma Christi 107
Pandion haliaetus 83, 84
    P. miliaceum 141, 142
Panthera leo 50
Papiobabuin 4
papyrus 125, 171, 172
partridge 5, 64
Passer domesticus 77
peacock 4
Pediculus humanus 36
pelican 19, 61, 65
Pelicanus onocrotalus 65
Phalacrocorax 18
Phoenician juniper 162
Phoenix dactylifera 160, 161
pig 80-81
pigeon 23
pine 99, 116, 123, 134, 162-164
Pinus brutia 164;
    P. halepensis 129, 162, 163
piscis 27-29
pistachio 164, 165
Pistacia lentiscus 93, 94, 95;
    P. palaestina 165, 182;
    P. terebinthus 182, 183;
    P. vera 164, 165, 182
plane tree 165, 166-167
Platanus orientalis 166, 167
poison 167-168
pomegranate 168-170
poplar 169, 170, 178
Populus alba 178;
    P. euphratica 169, 170
porcupine 66
porpoise 22
Poterium spinosum 184, 185
Procavia syriacus 69
Prunus armeniaca 92
Pterocarpus santalinus 88
Pulex irritans 29

pumpkin 106
Punica granatum 168
purple heron 41
purslane 170-171
pygarg 2

quail 66-67
Quercus aegilops 154, 155;
    Q. coccifera 154, 155;
    Q. ilex 128, 129

rabbit 39, 70
ram 20, 75
Rana punctata 32, 33
rat 57
raven 24, 67-69
red deer 20
red lily 135
red tulip 150
reed 125, 130, 171-174
Retama raetam 100, 101
Ricinus communis 106, 107
rock badger 69
rock goat 38, 76
rock partridge 64
rock rabbit 70
rock rose 60
roe deer 20, 26
rooster 16, 17
rose 150, 151, 178, 187
rose of Jericho 187
rose of Sharon 150
Rubus sanctus 186
rue 173, 174
Rumex acetocella 89
rush 125, 171, 174
Ruta chalepensis 174;
    R. graveolens 173, 174

Sabina phoenicia 108
Saccharum officinarum 173
saffron 174-175
Salix alba 170
Salsola kali 188
saltwort 101, 136
Salvadora persica 146
sandalwood 88, 110
sandarac 109-110
sand gecko 35
sand lizard 52
sand partridge 5, 64

[207]

Index of Greek Terms

aetos 82,84,85

agrielaios 156

aigeios 36,38

akantha 184,186

akanthinos 184,186

akris 53,54

alektōr 16,17

aleuron 195,197

aloē 90

alōpēx 31,32

amnos 75,76

ampelōn 188

ampelos 188

anēthon 117

apsinthos 198

arēn 75,76

arkos 8,9

arnion 75,76

aspis 72,73

batos 184,186

batrachos 33

botanē 125,126

botrus 188,191

bous 62,63

bussos 119,121

choiros 80,81

cholē 198

chortos 125,126

damalis 62,63

echidna 72,73,74

elaia 156,157

enalia 27,28

eriphion 36,38

eriphos 36,38

gleukos 188,191

gups 83

hēduosmon 143

herpeton 72,73

hippos 43,45

hupozugion 5,7

hus 80,81

hussōpos 129,130

ichthudion 27,28

ichthus 27,28

kalamē 171,172

kalamos 171,172

kamelos 13,14

keration 103

kētos 27,28,29

kinnamōmon 108,109

kōnōps 35,36

korax 67,68

krinon 134,135,136

krithē 95,96

krithinos 96

ktēnos 62,63

kuminon 114,115

kunarion 21,22

kuōn 21,22

kuparissos 123

lachanon 125,126

leōn 50,51

libanos 121,122

linon 119,120,121

lukos 85,86

manna 139,141

moron 145

moschos 62,63

nardos 151,152

nossia 16,17

nossion 16,17

oinos 188,191

olunthos 118,119

onarion 5,7

onos 5,7

ophis 72,73

opsarion 27,28

ornis 16

othonia 119,120,121

oxos 192

pardalis 48,49

pascha 75,76

pēganon 174

peristera 23,24

phoinix 160,162

pōlos 5,7

probation 75,76

probaton 75,76

prosphagion 27,28

semidalis 195,197

sēs 55,56

sikera 188,191

sinapi 145

sindōn 119,121

sition 197

sitista 62,63

sitos 195,197

skōlēx 86

skolops 186

skorpios 70,71

smurna 147,148

staphulē 188,191

strouthion 77

sukaminos 144,145,182

sukē 118,119

sukomorea 179,181

sukon 118,119

tauros 62,63

thremma 62,63

thuinos 109,110

tragos 36,38

tribolos 184,186

trugōn 24

zizanion 194

Index of Terms from Other Languages

Akkadian

da-as-su 3

rīmu 63

Arabic

birbir 39

dara'a 43

gharab 170

mann 139

ratam 100

rim 63

Assyrian

kukanitu 107

Egyptian

gf 4

kiki 107

ky 4

p-ih-mw 12

ths 22

Latin

posca 192

talpa 55

Sanskrit

picita 152

Syriac

dadar 165

Index of Hebrew and Aramaic Terms

dishon 2,3,46

dobh 8,9

dohan 141,142

dudha?im 138

dukhiphath 42

?ebheh 171,172

'eghel 62

'eghlah 62

?eghoz 192

?el 162

?elah 154,182,183

?eleph 62,63

?elon 154,155,183

'enabh 188,191

?eph'eh 72,73

'erebh 170

?erez 108

'esebh 125

?eshel 182

?eshkol 162,191

?eshkol 'anabim 188

?eshkol hagephen 188

'ets-'abhoth 149

'ets shemen 156,157

?etun 120

'ez 36,38

?ezobh 129,130

?ezrah 133,134

gadh 110

galgal 187

gamal 13,14

gazam 53

gebh(-im) 53

gedhi 36,38

gephen 188,190

gobhay 53,54

gome? 171

gopher 123

gor 50,51

gozal 23,24

gur 50,51

habharburoth 49

habhatstseleth 150

hadhas 149

haghabh 53,54

hallamuth 170

hamor 5,6

hapharparah 54

hargol 53,54

harul 152

hashash 125

hasidhah 78

hasil 53,54

hatsir 125,126,159,160

hazir 80,81

hedheq 184,185

helbenah 123,149

hemer 188,190

hittah 195,197

hoah 184,185,186

hobhnim 117

holedh 55

homet 16,52

homets 192

?i 31,32,46

?immar 75,76

kammon 114,115,117

kar 75,76

karkom 174,175

karpas 111,112

kebhes 75,76

kelebh 21

ken 36

kephir 50,51

kerem 188,190

kopher 127

kinnam 35,36

kinnim 35,36

kippah 160

kirkaroth 13,14

koah 35,52

kos 51,61

kussemeth 175

kussemim 175

la'anah 198

labhi? 50

layish 50,51

lebhi (-?im) 50,192

lebonah 121,122

leta?ah 35,52

libhneh 178

lilith 59,62

liwyathan 72,73,74

lot 147,148,149,178

luz 89,90

malluah 136,137

man 139,141

mashqeh 188,190

merorim 98

mesukah 186

mesukah 186

mesukkah 184,186

mezeg 188,191

miqshah 113

mor 147,148

na'atsuts 184,185

nahal 162

nahash 72,73

namer 48,49

nataph 178

nemalah 1

nemar 49

nerd 151,152

neshar 82,84

nesher 82,83,84

nets 40,41

'opher 20

'orebh 67,68

?oren 108,133,134

'ozniyah 82,83,84,85

pag 118,119

paqqu'oth 124

par 62

parah 62

parash 43,45

par'osh 29

peqa?im 125

pere? 5,7

peredh 57,58

peres 82,83,84

pesheth 119,120

pethen 72,73

pirdah 57,58

pishtah 119,120

pol 97

qa?ath 19,41,61,65

qaneh 171,172

qaphaz 4

qerets 33

qetsah 117,153

qetsi'oth 104,105

qiddah 104,105

qimmosh 184,186

qinnamon 108,109

qippodh 66

qippoz 4,5,62,64

qiqayon 106,107

qishshu? 112,113

qoph 4

qore? 64

qots 184,186

ra'ah 40,41

raham 82,83,84

rahel 75,76

re'em 63

rekhesh 43,45,58

renanim 60,61

rimmah 86

rimmon 168

rosh 167

ro'sh 167,198

rothem 100,132

sa'ir 36,38

sarigh 188,190

sas 55,56

seh 36,38,75,76

se'irah 36,38

sekh 184,186

sekhwi 16,17

selaw 66

semamith 52,78

seneh 184,185,186

se'orah 95,96

shabbelul 76

shahal 50,51

shahaph 61,71

shahats 51

shakh 57

shalakh 18,61

shamir 184,186

shaphan 69

shaqedh 89,90

sharaph 72,73

shayith 184,186

sheheleth 60,149

shekhar 188,190

shemer 188,191

shephiphon 72,73

shiqmah 179,181,182

shittah 87

shor 62

shoshan 134,136

shoshannah 134,136

shu'al 31,32

shum 159

shushan 134,135,136

siah 137

sikera 188

sillon 184,185,186

sir 184,185,186

sirpadh 184,185

sis 80

sobhe' 188,190,192

sol'am 53,54

soreq 188,190,191

soreqah 188,190

suph 171

sus (1) 24,80

sus (2) 43,45

tahash 22,38

tahmas 59,61

taleh 75,76

tamar 160,162

tan (-nim) 31,32,74

tannin 72,73,74

tappuah 92,93

tayish 36,38

te'ashshur 99,115,116

te'enah 118,119

te'o 3,46,47,63

tidhhar 128,164,165,167

timorah 160,162

tinshemeth 15,51,55,61

tirosh 188,191

tirzah 116,128

Index of Bible References

[216]

2 Chronicles (cont.)	
33.11	185,186

Ezra	
2.66-67	6
6.9,17	76
7.17	76
8.35	38

Nehemiah	
1.11	190
2.13	73
4.3	32
5.11	191
7.68-69	6
8.15	149,157
9.20	141
10.37,39	191
13.5,12	191
13.15	191

Esther	
1.6	112
2.12	148
8.10	45,58
8.14	45,58
8.15	112

Job	
3.8	73,74
4.10	51
4.11	50,51
4.19	50
5.5	186
6.5	7,125
6.6	171
7.5	86
7.12	73
8.11	125,171
8.14	78
9.26	84,172
10.16	51
11.12	6,7
13.28	56
17.14	86
20.14	73
20.16	72,73,167,168
21.26	86
24.5	7
24.20	86

Job (cont.)	
24.24	137
25.6	86
27.18	56
28.7	12,41
28.8	51
29.18	162
30.1	21
30.4	100,137
30.7	152
30.29	32
31.22	173
31.40	185,195
38.27	125
38.36	17
38.39	50
38.41	68
39	61
39.1	20
39.5	7
39.9	63
39.13	41,61,79
39.26	41
39.27	84
40.15	12
40.17	12
40.21	172
40.22	170
41	74
41.1	73,74
41.2	171,174,185,186
41.20	171,174

Psalms	
8.7	63
17.8	93
18.33	20
18.36	43
22 (title)	20
22.12	63
22.16-21	21
22.16,20	21
22.21	63
23.2	125
29.6	63
29.9	20
37.2	125
37.35	133,134
39.11	56
42.1	20

Psalms (cont.)	
44.19	32
45	136
45.8	90,104,105,148
50.10	63
50.13	63
51.7	130
52.8	156
55.6	24
57.4	50
58.4	73
58.8	77
58.9	185
59.6,14	21
60	136
63.10	32
68.23	21
68.30	172
69	136
69.12	190
69.21	168,192,198
72.9	46
73.22	12
74.13	73
74.14	46,73
75.8	191
78.24	141
78.45	33
78.46	54
78.47	181
80	136
80.10	189
83.11	86
83.13	188
84.3	77,80
90	125
91.13	51,73
92.10	63
102.6	52,65
102.17	132
103.5	84
104.11	7
104.17	79,163
104.18	46,70
104.26	73,74
105.30	33
105.31	36
105.34	54
105.40	67

1 Corinthians (cont.)		Revelation	
15.37	197	1.14	76
15.39	28,63	2.17	141
		4.7	51,63, 85
2 Corinthians			
11.3	73	5.5	50,51
12.7	186	6.2,4,5	45
		6.6	96,191, 197
Ephesians			
5.18	191	6.8	45
		6.13	119
Philippians		7.9	162
3.2	22	8.7	126
		8.11	198
1 Timothy		8.13	85
3.8	191	9.3	54,71
5.18	63	9.4	126
5.23	191	9.5	70,71
		9.7	45,54
2 Timothy		9.8	51
4.17	51	9.9	45
		9.10	70,71
Hebrews		9.17	45,51
6.7	126	9.19	45,73
6.8	186	10.3	51
9.4	141	11.1	172
9.12	38,63	11.4	157
9.13	38,63	12.9	73
9.19	38,63,130	12.14	73,85
10.4	38,63	13.2	9,49,51
11.33	51	14.8,10	191
11.37	38	14.18	191
		14.20	45,190
James		15.6	121
1.10	126	16	33
1.11	126	16.13	33
3.3	45	16.19	191
3.7	28,73	17.2	191
3.12	119	18.3	191
5.2	56	18.13	45,63, 109,122, 197
1 Peter			
1.19	76	19.11,14	45
1.24	126	19.15	191
5.8	51	19.18,19, 21	45
2 Peter		20.2	73
2.16	7	21.16	172
2.22	22	22.15	22,172
3 John			
v. 13	172,174		